CW00433238

Penguin Books

Visible Panty Line

Gretel Killeen is a writer, performer, journalist, voice artist, humorist, public speaker and mother. In short, she is a High Achiever, despite dropping out of law school. Gretel has written and performed for Triple J, 2MMM, Radio National, Regional ABC radio, and 2BL. She has also worked extensively in television, whether as a horse's bottom for the Melbourne Cup, as Ray Martin's wife (in *The Midday Show* soapie send-up 'A Town Like Dallas'), a Beauty to Stan Zemanek's Beast on Foxtel's *Beauty and the Beast*, an outspoken guest loudmouth on *Mouthing Off* or, more recently, on the Channel Nine Super Debates and *Good News Week*.

After starting in stand-up comedy, Gretel became co-producer of Comics in the Park and Actors in the Park at Sydney's former landmark performance venue, the Harold Park Hotel. As co-writer, performer and producer of *Oz Rap*, she won a Penguin Award.

Gretel Killeen's column appeared weekly for two years in *The Australian Magazine*. She is the author of numerous best-selling children's books and lives in Sydney with her two children, Zeke and Eppie – whose first books were published in 1999.

Also by Gretel Killeen

Baby on Board
How to Live With a Sausage in a Bonnet
Every Girl's Geek Guide
My Life Is a Toilet
The My Life Is a Toilet Instruction Book
The My Life Is a Toilet Diary
Cherry Pie
What'll We Get For Grandma
My Sister's a Yoyo
My Sister's an Alien
My Sister's a Sea Slug
My Sister's a Burp

visible
panty line

Gretel Killeen

Penguin Books

Penguin Books Australia Ltd
487 Maroondah Highway, PO Box 257
Ringwood, Victoria 3134, Australia
Penguin Books Ltd
Harmondsworth, Middlesex, England
Penguin Putnam Inc.
375 Hudson Street, New York, New York 10014, USA
Penguin Books Canada Limited
10 Alcorn Avenue, Toronto, Ontario, Canada M4V 3B2
Penguin Books (NZ) Ltd
Cnr Rosedale and Airborne Roads, Albany, Auckland, New Zealand
Penguin Books (South Africa) (Pty) Ltd
5 Watkins Street, Denver Ext 4, 2094, South Africa
Penguin Books India (P) Ltd
11, Community Centre, Panchsheel Park, New Delhi 110 017, India

First published by Penguin Books Australia 1999

5 7 9 10 8 6

Copyright © Gretel Killeen 1999

All rights reserved. Without limiting the rights under copyright reserved
above, no part of this publication may be reproduced, stored in or intro-
duced into a retrieval system, or transmitted, in any form or by any means
(electronic, mechanical, photocopying, recording or otherwise), without
the prior written permission of both the copyright owner and the above
publisher of this book.

Design and digital imaging by Anitra Blackford, Penguin Design Studio
Cover photograph by Tim De Neefe
Text illustration by Chris Bellamy
Typeset in 11/15pt Apollo by Post Pre-press Group, Brisbane, Queensland
Printed in Australia by Australian Print Group, Maryborough, Victoria

National Library of Australia

Cataloguing-in-Publication data:

Killeen, Gretel.
Visible panty line.

ISBN 0 14 028891 0.

1. Killeen, Gretel – Anecdotes. 2. Killeen, Gretel – Humor.
3. Australian newspapers – Sections, columns, etc.
4. Australian wit and humor. 5. Australia – Social life and
customs – 20th century. I. Title. II. Title: Australian
magazine (Surry Hills, N.S.W.: 1988).

070.444

www.penguin.com.au

To my mother and father, who gave me life twice,
and to Z and E, who give me life endlessly.

contents

live by the

motto carpe diem:

a fish a day

superwoman

What am I going to do today? Oh, first I think I'll sleep in and not bounce out of bed 'til dawn.

Then I'll jog 8 kilometres, swim another 50, dry myself off with a fluffy white towel and balance my vitamin pills on my pert, firm breasts.

At 6, after I've washed, toned, moisturised my supple body, and removed all excess hair, I'll wake my magnificently handsome, wealthy, caring and yet well-hung husband. We'll make love and both reach orgasm. In fact, I'll probably reach several.

We'll weigh ourselves, I'll practise my golf swing, he'll manicure his nails, we'll both sing 'Nessun Dorma'. We'll share some Swedish muesli and compare our bowel movements, then I'll do my pelvic floor exercises while we discuss The Aussie Dollar. We'll weigh ourselves, make love, have another orgasm.

Then I'll realign the distributor of his turbo-charged Range Rover, say something supportive, encouraging, sympathetic and witty, kiss him goodbye, have another orgasm, and watch him drive off to his high-powered yet environmentally sensitive occupation.

At 7.30 I'll go to wake our two beautiful children and probably find them making their beds and folding their clothes. I'll vacuum their rooms as we cuddle.

Then I'll marvel at such maturity in four- and six-year-olds as Jaaaack checks the All Ordinaries Index and Isabellar makes a 35-mm, feature-length film of herself and our neighbour, Elle Macpherson, preparing pâté and sprout sandwiches for play lunch.

We'll send some homemade bagels to Ethiopia by courier. Nelson Mandela will ring to say hi, Bill Gates will call for my advice, then I'll bundle the kids into my Range Rover and drive them off to their private school where the teachers not only comment on how clean and bright their uniforms are but enquire after the brand of my washing powder.

At the lights I'll read *The Financial Review*, touch up my lippy, do *The Times'* crossword and perform a citizen's arrest upon a well-known international terrorist, drug smuggler and defaulter of child-maintenance payments.

I'll enter my office at 8.25 to level-headedly pursue my high-profile career as a successful, respected, financially well-rewarded home carer, Marilyn Monroe lookalike and neurosurgeon.

I'll make a dillion dollars, climb Mount Everest at lunchtime (with no oxygen), have a beer with the local homeless people in the park, and then ring my mum to say, 'I love you'. At 2 I'll shop for groceries, give 40 litres of blood, tie up some deals in London and Japan and power walk to the toilet.

At 3, I'll be offered a pay rise, 4 a promotion, at 5 I'll take over the firm. Then I'll find a bird with a broken wing, heal it, watch it fly away, win three sets on the court, and pick up the kids from Tae Kwon Do, the Young Republicans, their personal trainers or analysts.

At 6 I'll whip up a little five-course something (vichyssoise, sashimi, coq au vin, zabaglione, Tarte au Magnifique), help Jaaaack hack into NASA, teach Isabellar to *feeeeeeeeel* Rachmaninov, give myself a facial, do the family accounts, and assist the woman at the corner shop to give birth.

At 6.25 my husband will come home from colonic irrigation carrying the fatted calf he killed on our property only this arvo using nothing but his bare teeth. I'll give him a massage from 6.30 to 7 and afterwards we'll make long and passionate love for a few minutes on the floor.

We'll have an orgasm and then I'll relax as I wash and iron until the seven influential guests and their attractive young wives arrive.

We'll discuss politics, domestic help, superannuation, our retirements in Tuscany, poor people, and our years in Provence until 1 or maybe 2 in the morning when they'll leave in their jets and I'll clear up, wash up, put away, make the kids' lunches, press the kids' uniforms, shine the kids' school shoes, finish the kids' homework and take Roland our Great Dane for a perve at girl dogs in the park.

At 3.45 I'll paint an oil portrait of Jaaaack and Isabellar for my forthcoming exhibition at the Louvre, read *Ulysses* (in Latin), and write a chapter of my thesis on synchronic elaboration of semiotic nuclei.

And then . . .
at 4,
I'll do 300 push ups,

turn out the light,
climb into bed,
and make love to my husband.

Oh, I'll probably fake that orgasm. But I'll certainly do it extremely well.

the weak that was

Saturday

Early morning, I see a sign on an enormous construction site near our home. It is self-promotion for the developers with bold, enormous writing that wraps itself all the way round the scaffolding until it runs out of space. 'GARVAC,' it reads, big strong and proud, 'PLANNING FOR THE FUT'.

My six-year-old daughter doesn't want to play footy today. My son has told her she's going to get her head kicked in because she's the only girl. I convinced her to join the team by telling her she looks beautiful in her uniform. I encourage the kids not to get too involved in the game; to avoid rough tackles and dives to the ground. The kids think I am being caring and protective. I just don't want to have to wash their footy jerseys.

Sunday

10 a.m., I'm at the shops and my bum drops. I've heard this happens to women as they get older but I always thought it would be a gradual process, not like suddenly rising from a chair and realising the cushion has adhered itself to the back of your thighs. Now I'm feeling old and frail. I start telling people I'm eighty-seven, so they think I look young for my age. I buy myself a pair of butt-lifting jeans. The assistant tells me that because jeans stretch I

should buy them two sizes too small. The jeans are so tight I have a headache from the blood that's rushed to my head.

Monday

Driving the kids to school, I look in the rear-vision mirror and notice black smoke billowing from the back of the car. I decide the best way to make it go away is to stop looking in the rear-vision mirror. I go to the nearest petrol station. The mechanic looks at the engine and finally says with scathing ridicule, 'Jesus, who serviced her last?' 'You did,' I reply.

Tuesday

My children decide they want to change their names to Princess Aurora and Kevin. My daughter calls my son 'boy's bra', which apparently is horribly offensive. Someone breaks into my car, rips out the radio, and then, disappointed with its quality, throws the radio away. I know this because I find it later that day hurled into my neighbour's garden.

My mother arrives with an old brass flower pot with vines scratched on the side. 'I was going to throw this out,' she says, 'but it reminded me so much of you.' Dad says Mum will be offended if I don't accept it. Years of familial scabs are picked. I am reminded of American satirist Stephen Pearl saying, 'I phoned my dad to tell him I'd stopped smoking, and he called me a quitter.'

Wednesday

For the third night in a row my healthy daughter says she's too sick to do her reading. I tell her she has to do her reading or I will be forced to go in and chat with her teacher. We are at a teary impasse until Eppie comes up with a solution: 'I know,' she says, 'you read to me, and I'll tell you if you're right.'

Thursday

Winter arrives with a bang. I go to play sparrows' twit golf for the first time in my life. I get to the course, it is absolutely freezing, I run home to put on my ski suit. I wonder why people bother to play golf when the golf cart is so much more fun. I wonder whether the two activities can't be incorporated – eradicate golf as we know it and invent Golf Cart Polo.

I call the mechanic who tells me I should get a new car because this one has had its day. He says the car has no value at all but he will offer me $200 cash; apparently it's how much loose change he found between the seats.

Friday

I'm suffering a great deal from writer's block and thinking of getting the euthanasia program installed into my word processor. SAVE? CANCEL? EUTHANASIA?

A close friend rings. She's absolutely devastated because she and her husband have just split up over a horrible argument about what they will do with their enormous Lotto winnings. Not only have they not won Lotto, they also don't play it. She says she thinks they should go to a relationship counsellor but her husband is very busy. Do I think it's tragic, she asks, 'to go to a relationship counsellor by yourself?'

Everything is getting a bit too hard. The toilet empties every time we empty the bath, the man who was coming to fix the washing machine apparently died on an earlier job. I ask my kids what they think the meaning of life is. My son says he thinks it's living. My daughter asks if she can have all my clothes when I die.

Later that night I read a little something by US humorist Ronnie Shakes that helps put it into perspective. 'After 12 years of therapy, my psychiatrist said something that brought tears to my eyes. He said, *"No hablo inglés"*.'

Saturday

To be continued . . .

stuffing stuff

I'm holding an old white tennis sock, which I've stuffed with odd balls of wool. I've tied a knot at one end of the sock, and drawn two black dots on the other. 'There,' I say. 'Does that look like a harp seal?'

'No,' says my son Zeke, in tears. 'Well, it will when I add the wings.' 'Mum, harp seals don't have wings.' 'Look at the photo, what are those things on the side then?' 'They're flippers.' 'Well, we'll make flippers and we'll use cardboard and I'll glue them on and then it will look like a harp seal.' (I do this. It takes one hour and forty-five minutes, seventeen different prototypes and costs $8.70 in cardboard.) 'How will we join the flippers on?' asks Zeke. 'We'll use glue.' We have seven types of glue in our house. None is suitable for glueing cardboard to a tennis sock. Six dollars fifty later, the wing-like flippers are attached to the sock-like seal. 'But the flippers are hard, and the rest of the body is soft,' says Zeke. 'Well, we'll cover them with cotton wool.'

Luckily our corner shop sells cotton wool for emergencies like this. A simple roll cost a mere $2751. 'Do you think we should get two, Mum, in case we make a mistake?' 'We won't make a mistake Zekie, we know what we're doing now.' Two hours later, we're back at the shop, buying another roll. The wing-flipper-things now look like some sad old Santa hat the cat dragged in. There's an idea. 'Why not take the cat in, it's white. Just tuck his tail down and hold his legs really close to his body . . .' (Time passes.)

'Okay then, why don't we stuff an old Santa hat and bleach the red bits white?' I'm on a roll. After the Santa hat, we try dyeing a feather duster, painting a raw pork sausage, papier-mâchéing two balloons ('Yes, Zeke, harp seals can be completely round.'). Finally I suggest a base-ball bat with tomato sauce on the end. 'Mum, that's not a harp seal.' 'It's a grown-up socio-political comment and I'm sure your teacher will think it's fabulous.'

Zeke whimpers. He appears to be losing the power of speech. A neighbour drops by, an architect showing uncharacteristic sensitivity to our domestic circumstances for someone who allows his dog to poo on the pavement outside our front door at least once a day. He constructs something using bits of wood and tiles from the dump bin up the road. When he's finished, his harp seal looks like the dump bin up the road.

Zeke is almost hysterical. 'Zeke,' I say, wondering whether I should repeat the lecture about this is your project and you've known about it for three weeks and you have to learn to be responsible for your own homework, 'Why don't you paint a harp seal?' 'I can't.' 'Of course you can, just get a piece of cardboard from the pile of scraps over there and draw two black dots on it and call it "Harp Seal in a Snow Storm".' 'I don't want to.'

A day of my life has passed; I've aged twenty-three years. My hair has gone completely white, my skin is pale and wan. 'Why don't you take me to school?' I say. 'I look like a harp seal.' My son doesn't answer. He's falling into a coma.

'Zeke, do you have to make a harp seal? Can't we make a different animal?' 'Okay.' 'Oh good,' I say, eyeing a strand of wool. 'Why don't we make a worm?' 'Someone's already done that.' (Aha, so someone's parents are smarter than I. We'll see about that.) 'How about an amoeba? We'll just take the ball of plasticine that was going to be a harp seal's head . . .' 'No.' 'All right, well what animal can you make, Zeke, a lion?' 'Been done.' (Gee that's an advanced mother!) 'A horse?' 'Been done.' (The standard of parents in this class is definitely 'gifted'.) 'Well, what hasn't been done?' 'A giraffe.' 'Do you want to make a giraffe?' I say. 'Yes,' says Zeke as 10 p.m. Sunday approaches and he flops upstairs to bed.

Monday morning: Zeke dribbles down the stairs. To his delight, a giraffe and African tree have appeared on the kitchen table. 'Wow Mum, thanks.' Monday afternoon: 'How did you go Zeke?' 'The teacher said that if I made it, it was very good, but if you made it, the tree was the wrong sort and the giraffe looked like a long-necked pony.' Oh no, I panic, so he *knows* I made it then. 'Did you get into trouble?' 'No. He said I don't get a gold star for aptitude but I get a Bart Simpson stamp for delegation.'

(Editor's note: Gretel gained a mark of 48/50 for her giraffe. We think she can do better.)

legends of the sea

The last time I saw Spew he was drinking beer and cigarette butts from an overflowing ashtray as the pub crowd roared 'skol, skol'. We were both fifteen then; now we're both thirty-four, and I'm standing on the wharf watching this stockbroking, union-playing, balding father of three load a 14-metre rental yacht with so much grog there's no room for his kids. 'It doesn't really matter,' he says through ciggy-clasping teeth, 'we've got an excellent Swedish au pair and she's surprisingly reliable for someone with such a good bod.'

Blonde wife, Lou, legend for skolling a bottle of Kahlua at fourteen and vomiting on the then-prime minister, is on board unpacking the grog, chooks and pot. She stashes the pot in the first-aid box which is otherwise full of emergency anti-wrinkle cream and depilatory lotion.

She shows me some photos of the kids. Shot by a professional photographer, everyone thinks the kids look just gorgeous. In fact, they're hardly recognisable. Lou's on the boat with all her old school chums: Sal, Nicky, Vick, Cath, Jen, and Gin, who luckily are all married to Spew's old schoolmates: Hog, Hose Monster, Fatman, Big Balls, Mullet, and Half a Yard of Mackerel Salami.

At last we're ready to take off, and to celebrate Mullo rolls an enormous joint. The crew spends the next hour-

and-a-half laughing at their boating shoes and trying to stick their tongues up their noses. Hilarious. *Sizzling Seventies* plays on the stereo, the first few slabs of beer are quaffed, the first poofter joke is told, and the first 'while you're down there' said to a female bending over to collect something from the cabin floor.

Hose Monster, famous not just for the glaringly obvious but also for once mowing the shag pile carpet at a wedding reception that he gatecrashed, stands on the cabin roof chucking brown-eyes at a passing police launch. Everyone finds this absolutely 'hysterical' and makes a mental note to file the incident under 'legend' to recall readily and repeatedly later.

Drink, drink, drink.

Big Balls is practising his golf swing on the bow and drives one straight into Fatman who was trying to score a bit of sex by reciting the names of all the original *Get Smart* cast members to Vicky's sister, Nicky. Fatman falls into the water and Nicky dives in to save him. When Fatman recovers, Nicky's lost interest. Why, what is she? Gay? No-one else cares; this is fantastic, two legends already and it's not even two o'clock.

Drinking games commence. The favourite is mentally exhausting but well worth the effort. It's called 'stack' and what you have to do is pile everything on the table into a stack, and the person who makes it collapse has to skol his choice of spirit. At a quarter to four Big Balls throws up into what he thinks is the sea, but is in fact the hatch to the queen bed cabin. Jen is spinning out in the bed at the time. Another legend. Cool.

'My Sharona' comes on: those who can stand perform the famous dance of the creative two beats to the right, two beats to the left, nod your head to the music, bite your top lip. This dance makes Mullo's wife, who actually has no other name, very hungry so she goes downstairs to heat some taco shells on a plastic dish and after forty minutes manages to set the cabin on fire. Unreal. Another legend.

Hog dry-humps the mast and asks it to marry him, all the girls giggle charmingly and Half a Yard, taking a leak over the side, turns to see what's so funny and sprays them. They scream 'oh yuk', but are really glad to at last have some attention.

Time passes. Bottles, cans, Ginny and Big Balls go overboard. Cath burps the alphabet. Hog sings rugby songs with Sal. Then Sal lights one of Hog's farts, which, in a feat of superhuman endeavour, travels so very far it makes a gas cylinder explode in a neighbouring boat. Excellent. Another legend!

Everyone's getting a little tired now. It's been a long and hard day. Spew's suffering from not having made an ill-informed and irresponsible decision with a large amount of money since the sharemarket closed on Friday. He's betting that Hose Monster can't stand up, but he does so Spew loses $30,000. Legend number five. A Royal Flush. And we haven't even left the mooring!

It starts to rain. It's five o'clock. That's the cocktail hour. Adjourn to the pub to relive the moments and recall the wacky people that we are.

sex and sexability

There's not nearly enough sex in my life and I'm blaming the Barina. Of course, being single with two children doesn't help – but then being married with children didn't help either.

I haven't had a good sex life while owning the Barina because the Barina doesn't make me feel sexy. Anything that's designed to be practical and efficient is not going to reek sexuality. For eleven years I was content to zip and dart through life, tiny and unnoticed, but now I'm no longer satisfied with small. All of a sudden I want huge. I don't want a car that goes 'beep beep' anymore. I want a car that moans. Actually I don't just want a car that moans and groans, I want a whole life that does. I want absolutely everything within my realm to ooze profound sexuality. Not sex, mind you, I'm over that. I've played needle in a haystack long enough. Indeed my last even vaguely sexual experience was in 1989 when I wore a G-string to aerobics.

So I'm wanting sexuality, not sex. There is a vast distinction between sex and sexuality, and it's not explained at all by the following joke. What's the difference between a clitoris and a golf ball? A man will spend at least thirty minutes looking for a golf ball.

Sex is grunt and rub and check the ceiling for cobwebs,

while sexuality (herein also referred to as sexy and sexual) is charisma, taste, indulgence and confidence. Sex is about 'Do you wanna? Nah.' While sexuality is all about using the words fab and divine and absolutely gorgeous.

Leading a sexy, sexual life is about finding the drag queen within. It's about saying exactly what you think, very, very loudly and with lots and lots of gush. It's about big laughter, big bosoms and big appetites. Sexuality's about having balls. It's about outrageousness, it's about honesty, it's about feeling and expressing and sharing and caring. It's about saying 'green salads suck'.

Sexuality's about not being polite.

Sexuality is all about breaking rules, which would explain why Australian society today is about as sexy as a ball of green snot. It's pretty hard to be effusive and wild in this constricted, repressed and anal society where new rules are made moment by moment to make the lily-livered feel safe. Sexuality is about generosity of spirit, it's about arrogance and *joie de vivre*, and to tell you the truth right at this time, it's precisely what this country needs.

The only humps anyone in this country is getting are lying on the road to stop us speeding. This country is a bore. In the dinner party of life, you just wouldn't invite us. Who'd find Australia fascinating to sit next to? Um, Canada? No wonder we're not invited anywhere; as a nation we're the consummate bore. Invitations go to those who are sexy because they're elusive, rich, exotic, fun, or simply downright fearful. No-one gets invited anywhere of worth just because their clothes are neat and ironed.

Australia needs a makeover. We need to be big and

loud. We need to be bright and strong and simply scrumptious; Australia needs to come out. And what better time to do it than the coming Olympic Opening Ceremony. 'Come camping in Australia,' we'll say.

We need frocks, we need falsies, we need a new national costume, one with lots of sequins and lamé. We need to get rid of that vile yellow and green, which no one on earth could possibly look good in. We need perhaps a nice cerise, with black and a dash of silver. We need the pattern duplicated on the flag, made out of satin with a feather trim.

Forget Julie Anthony — as sweet as she is, let's get Nick Cave, or Frank Bennett. And as for the anthem, it's just got to go because it clearly makes us all depressed. Let's change the key and change the beat and lastly can the lyrics, which probably shouldn't be all that hard since no one in the country knows them anyway.

We'll invent our own haka 'cause that's a very sexy dance, and then instead of an opening ceremonial speech we'll have a moment's silence (to make us all seem mysterious and aloof). Finally, amid resounding applause, our leader, wearing nothing but a codpiece and a barbecue apron with breasts painted on it, will light the Olympic flame, but not the flame of an enormous torch, rather an enormous Sambucca.

Fabulous, gorgeous, let's give it a bash. Meanwhile I'll try to sell the Barina — it's eleven years old, the rego's up and the car really needs a good vacuum.

what do I know?

I was recently asked to chair a discussion on *Jane Eyre*. Being a Methodist, workaholic perfectionist, I decided that prior to standing before an audience of hundreds and espousing my heartfelt views I should probably read the book. I then discovered just how thick it was. On the understanding that nearly everyone studied *Jane Eyre* at school, I thought I'd just ask someone to tell me the story instead.

'Jane Eyre?' said Jenny from next door, 'Um, what else did she write?'

'Charlotte Brontë?' said Nici from the local cafe. 'Isn't she a dress designer?'

'*Jane Eyre*?' said Will, with whom I work. 'Never read it, couldn't care less, it's a chick's book.' (Disappointed and gratuitously offended, I told him as I left his office about the planned sequel to that famous chick's movie, *The Piano*. 'It's a bloke's movie,' I said. 'It's about life from a male perspective, and it's going to be called *The Organ*.')

With time running ever shorter, my search became desperate. A cab driver told me he wanted to marry Jane Eyre: 'The book's about a poor girl who goes to a seminary, is treated unkindly, has one friend, friend dies of TB (or similar ailment), Jane hides away into herself, secures a job as a governess to the ward of an absentee landlord . . . da de da. Time passes, things happen . . .' I get out of the cab.

I saw the latest *Jane Eyre* movie in which the greatest special effect appears to be getting Elle Macpherson to look like she can act. I found an old, old friend. 'Tania, was *Jane Eyre* on your syllabus at school?'

'Yes.'

'Could you possibly tell me the story?'

'No, but if you ring Mum she can. She read all my books for me at school and wrote my essays as well.'

'God, I wish I'd studied *Jane Eyre* at school.'

'Well, that's funny,' said Tania, ''cause you did.'

I have no recollection of this. In fact, I have since realised, I have virtually no recollection whatsoever of anything I learnt at school. I remember dropping out of Law after six weeks because I couldn't find the exam room. And I remember dropping out of Communications when I accidentally handed in an empty manila folder for my assignments and received top marks for creativity. Beyond that, little else. I have subsequently written a poem containing absolutely everything I learnt at school. It's thirteen lines long and begins with: 'Missers m, missers i, missers s s i, missers s s i, missers p p i, stump jump plough. Never paddle in the Amazon River if you have a cut on your leg because you will get eaten by piranhas', and ends with 'The area of something is the square on the something else, and you can't ride a stallion if you're going through puberty'.

This 'what the hell have I learnt in my life' crisis gave me cause to wonder if my kids are learning anything at school. Apparently my son has learnt a new joke: What did the zero say to the eight? Hey, nice belt. My daughter has learnt that 'On a cow farm, they chop the boys' willies off and turn the cows into deers'.

Do any of us learn anything at school that is of any use in life? Why on earth do we bother? I came across a book the other day, *Live and Learn And Pass It On* . . . (compiled by H. Jackson Brown Jnr) in which people from all over the place summarise what they've learnt in life. Highlights include: 'I've learned that people will obey almost any reasonable request except "Please remain seated until the captain has brought the aircraft to a complete stop at the gate".' 'I've learned that you should never jump out of a second-storey window using a sheet for a parachute.' 'I've learned that I am slightly suspicious of people who fill their offices with awards and pictures of their family.' And 'I've learned that when I eat fish sticks they make you swim faster because they're fish.'

Of course, all the really important lessons occur outside learning institutions. So I lay in bed last night, drinking a cup of tea and wondering what is the most important lesson I've learnt so far . . .

And I wondered, and I drank more tea, and I wondered, and I drank more tea, and I wondered, and I drank more tea, and I realised: 'Life is like needing to go to the toilet in the middle of the night. You really don't want to get up and do it. But you feel so much better when you have.'

the female unique

Aunty Dorothy's getting married . . . again. She's seventy-eight, this is wedding number seven, and she's sitting at her kitchen table having a ciggy and a cup of tea and eating a huge piece of ham-and-pineapple pizza. She's just been measured for her wedding dress sleeves: 3 metres of mauve taffeta in each. She's resurrecting the fabric from her last wedding dress, which apparently no longer fits due to hormones. 'I've got to recycle wherever I can, 'cause these weddings can cost a fortune,' Aunt Dorothy comments as she puts the finishing touches on the honeymoon hat that was a clutch bag in 1985.

'Isn't Neville going to pay for the wedding dress?' I ask.

'No, Neville can't,' Aunt Dorothy replies, 'you see, he's a feminist.'

'What?'

'You know, like Ray Martin.'

No, Aunty Dorothy, I haven't got a clue. No woman in my family has ever been a feminist, much less a bloke to boot. My mother still believes that sexual harassment is wearing a pair of tight underpants.

I grew up in the shadow of the Bay City Rollers, not the shadow of Germaine's hairy armpits. So I have to confess that, even though I am demographically of that tribe that went to

Women's Lib marches in macramé papooses, I was not read *The Female Eunuch* as a bedtime story by a father wearing magenta overalls and a frangipani in his beard. My mother works like a plough horse, has no income of her own, goes without so we can go with, is under-appreciated, under-indulged, and appears to be quite happy. I'm only now coming to terms with the fact that my mother must be a male chauvinist pig. And as for my father, no, he's not a feminist. Lovely as he is, the most sexually liberated thing my Dad's ever done is allow my mother to save up and buy a microwave.

'You know what I mean, don't you dear,' says Aunt Dorothy. 'You understand.'

No, Aunt Dorothy, I do not. What does it mean when a man says he's a feminist; is he not just weeing on my tree? (My thoughts are momentarily interrupted by my sexist daughter, who wants to show me the dolly dress she's made for her football.)

For a while there I was a fake feminist. I called my girl-friends 'mate', cut my hair short and wore clothes that used to be beanbag covers. And since then I've forced myself to read most of the turgid feminist tomes – or at least their dust jackets. But to be quite honest I prefer to read the books on feminist humour, largely because they're shorter.

Oh Aunty Dorothy, don't make me feel bad. I've got enough guilt to bear for single-handedly being the cause of the State's water shortage by cleaning my teeth with the tap running.

'So,' Aunty Dorothy goes on and on, 'do you know what I mean?'

No, Aunt Dorothy, you tell me. The only blokes I know who call themselves feminists do so to show they're gentle, respectful and understanding, in an effort to get more sex. The only impact women's rights have had on most blokes I know is that it means dating now costs half as much.

'When Neville says he's a feminist, dear, what he's actually saying is that he respects my rights as a woman.'

'Couldn't he say it with diamonds?' I ask as I help carve the frozen leftover wedding cake from marriage number four into neat, little slice-size pieces.

'No, darling, it's more substantial than that. It means that he recognises my right to work for equal pay and to have access to childcare.'

'Aunt Dorothy, your son's fifty-nine.'

'And he respects the fact that as a woman I have a mind, and I have opinions, and I should therefore not simply be treated as a sex object. And he recognises my right to put the garbage out, to enjoy the football and to be treated as his financial equal.'

'The sum total of which,' I reply, 'means he's generously letting you pay for your own wedding frock.'

'And the wedding.'

'You're paying for the entire wedding?'

'Yes. And I'm doing the flowers and I'm doing the catering and I'm doing the invites, and I'm organising seating, and I'm hiring the band.'

'Boy, Aunty Dorothy you must really want to get married!'

'No, dear, I think the whole thing's ridiculous. It's Neville who wants to tie the knot.'

'So why on earth are you going through all this?'

'Well, dear, because there's a lovely young altar boy I'd like to meet.'

last year's (super) model

I once caught a T-bar with an old Hungarian, who gave me some tips for my skiing: bend the knees, stocks in close, and, of course, most important of all, follow your breasts down the hill. 'Oh, that one's easy,' I said with glee, 'My breasts have faced downhill for years.'

'No,' she replied, 'your breasts must face straight ahead, and then you follow them down.'

'What, your breasts can't face downwards?'

'Oh no, not at all.'

'Well there goes that sport for me.'

'You could try following some other part of your body,' she said.

'No I can't,' I replied. 'If I followed any other part of this ever-spreading body I'd end up skiing sideways.'

So yes, the bod's going, going, gone, to that unfashionable retirement home under my kaftan, but do I feel bad about it at all? You bet your life I do. I'm even thinking of attending that psychotherapy group I Too Could Have Been a Rich Supermodel If I Wasn't So Completely Normal. Sure I can stare at Linda Evangelista and ask, 'Is she really happy?', but I can then also answer, 'Too bloody right she is.' And I'm not alone in my bitter, jealous corner. The only thing at the moment that keeps half the women in this country from committing harakiri with their calorie-laden mascara brushes is the current rampant rumour that our Elle might have cellulite.

I need a supermodel who relates to me; Hazel Hawke comes to mind. Sure, the others are gorgeous and 'so professional', but get some children and go sleepless for nine years and then tell me your complexion secrets. What I want to know is, when will dark circles from beneath your eyes to your navel become an accepted beauty statement? (Alice Cooper ignored at this point.)

But of course, the really big question among us girls still remains: 'Has Dannii Minogue had a facelift?' I say yes, of course she has. When you've given every other part of your body the lift, it's just logical your face is going to shift. Or, as a friend of mine recently pointed out, you end up with a very messy neckline.

Personally, I'm a fan of the knife and aspire to cosmetic surgery. I want to wear my knees as my bosoms, and my bosoms as my shoulder pads, and to feed a small nation with my thighs. (I wonder if that would make the op. tax deductible.) Like Cher I'm going to have half my body removed, although I'll probably stop at the brain.

I want a truly fashionable bod. Of course, I understand it could cost an arm and a leg, but I'm thinking of having my body parts sponsored. You know, these lips brought to you by Maryland Cherries, as opposed to this waist brought to you by Goodyear Tyres and these thighs by McDonald's.

I don't know what the problem is. I eat right and I exercise and I wash, tone and moisturise three times a day. I think I look particularly vile considering the effort I make. My son says just think how vile I'd look if I didn't.

Of course, it's a little bit bad for men, but not nearly as bad as for women. After all, a woman's role model is Helena Christensen, and a man's is Gerard Depardieu. I want to look fabulous in fashionable clothes that don't have baby vomit on the shoulders. I want heels that don't have to be sensible, and frocks that aren't made out of wipe and wear fabric or old Chux superwipes. Basically I want my old bosoms back. No, that's a lie, I want Claudia Schiffer's.

And I want to talk the fashionable talk. I want to say 'do lunch' and 'touch base' and 'I'll call you on the mobe', although I do draw the line at 'ciao'. I consider 'ciao' to be so pretentious I can't even bring myself to say it in Italia . . . sorry, Italy.

So what I want is a complete and utter makeover to make myself thoroughly fashionable. It's not going to be easy 'cause I'm genetically challenged and I come from a family of dags. We did try once to funk Mum up by buying her a pink smiley bag with matching yellow hot pants, but the whole project failed 'cause they aren't her colours, and she was sixty-five at the time.

But as I get older I hear the clock ticking and saying, 'Quick, get fashionable fast!' I'm getting old, not a moment to waste, the time to get hip is now because I certainly don't want to kick the bucket and have crowds of gawking strangers cry, 'Geez, I wouldn't be seen dead like that!'

save time, judge books

by their covers

when I grow up

A little friend of our family was recently discussing babies with us. If you have two, he said, they're called twins. If you have three, they're called triplets. And if you have four babies all at once, they're called cutlets.

Everything any child under the age of seven does or utters is cute, outrageous, quirky, brilliant and worth recording on video. But then something happens as we begin to age; humans go through subtle gear changes year after year until, by the age of thirty-five, we're all no longer exciting individuals but complete identikit bores. With this profound lack of colour and movement I don't know how they'll tell when we die.

What happens to us as we grow old? I bumped into an old schoolfriend who used to go by the nickname 'Animal' – not because he was strong and untamed but because he behaved like a pig. We laughed about our youth, the drugs, the drink, the sex, the parties, and then I asked, 'So what's new now?' He told me about the renovations and the advantages of his superfund.

How did this happen? Where did his spirit go? Was it when he married the bobbed blonde, or when he moved to the 'burbs, or has it happened all of a sudden now that the only approximation of sex the two of them experience together is castigating the family labrador for humping the couch?

Sure, we were wild and wacky in the old days, but wasn't everybody? We were meant to break rules. Now the wildest thing any of my peers do is wear Donald Duck motifs on their socks.

When does it happen that we transform from adventurous and interesting to a blancmange of untapped potential slouching on the settee? Does it start with that first pair of comfortable shoes and gain momentum with the first practical haircut? Or is it when you discover you're no longer eligible for a Kontiki Tour and looking good for a *Women's Weekly* Cruise?

Is this deterioration of 'oomph' genetic or is it simply learned? Can we possibly prevent it, or should we surrender? Can you postpone it by not having birthdays? It was my birthday the other day, and it was the worst one I've ever had. Of course, it wasn't helped by my not telling anyone, and then I got very upset when no one remembered. Oh no, I tell a lie, my accountant rang up and so did my lawyer, but I'll probably get bills for that next week.

My whole family forgot, and then, that morning, I got in a taxi and the vacant sign stayed up. Indeed, it wasn't until the following week that I gleaned any attention when my mother gave me a cosy foot-warmer and my kids gave me things that they'd like to have 'cause they figured they'll be inheriting them soon, anyway.

Am I fighting a losing battle, clinging to an invented, alternative *moi*?

You know you're getting old when you hear someone

died at 110 and think, 'Gee, that's young.' But do I have to be old? Do I have to lose my sense of humour? Do I have to play cards and stop cheating? Do I have to stop swearing and perving at boys? Do I have to wear my collar up at rugby matches?

In the film *Peter's Friends*, Kenneth Branagh quips: 'Adults are just children who owe money.' Which means what? That responsibility makes us bores? I think it is the fear of death that stops the adventurer within, but I don't think your path's any easier to heaven just because your shoes are clean. I think rebellion makes us all live longer, I think it makes your spirit stay alive. I think we should all sneak into movies without paying, quaff chocolate bars in the supermarket, wear heels we can't walk in, play music too loud, and stop thinking outrageous is putting some of your rubbish in a neighbour's otto bin.

Did you hear what happened when the Pope went to Heaven? God said: 'Welcome, and what would you like to do now that you're finally here?' And the Pope said: 'I'd like to go into the library and take a look at the very first Bible.' And so off the Pope went, terribly excited, but then came back a few hours later, dreadfully depressed. 'What's the matter?' asked God, and the Pope sobbed, 'Celebrate – I thought it was celibate!'

ode to Iphigenia

Spring is here. The birds are singing, the flowers are blossoming, feet are bared, and our spirits wake up to party. Spring is a time of smiles and laughter as the gentle breeze of change and hope plays upon our brows. Spring is a time of delight, joy and enthusiasm for all but one sad individual – Iphigenia (not her real name).

Iphigenia (not her real name) has lost her drive, her enthusiasm and an awful lot of weight. For three months she has spoken of nothing but the hopelessness of life and the bleakness of her future. Last week she announced she has made Misery her friend. Iphigenia has a broken heart.

(Did he drop her, did she drop him, did they drop each other at exactly the same time? These and other important questions will be answered after this short message from our sponsors: Kleenex tissues, Benson & Hedges, and skim-milk, decaf lattes.)

Eighty-seven days ago I told her, 'Never mind, there are plenty more fish in the sea.' And she replied, 'Yes I know, but they're all mullets, flatheads and gropers.'

Four days ago I announced, 'Enough is enough. It is better to have loved and lost than never to have loved at all.' And my good friend Iphigenia went to tell me that she appreciated my caring, my patience and my support. But she used only two words, and one of them was 'get'.

Some wise Roman, or perhaps a Spice Girl, once said, 'It is better that your ex-boyfriend spontaneously combusts than you be forced to go through the agony of a breakup.' And I must say that I'm starting to agree, because I'm finding all this dreadfully difficult. From morning 'til night my life is now filled with tears and sighs and staring into space, and that's just *my* behaviour.

Iphigenia (not her real name) is starting to make me sick. Love her to death, yes I do, but boring as bat poop, yes, she has become. And what amazes me more than anything else is the fact that I thought she was boring when she was with this bloke, so I never imagined she'd be so boring without him. Who would have thought I would long for the days of hearing all the nano-details of this man?

What has happened to my friend? Where is the girl who only last year thought the perfect partner could be adequately constructed out of a fruit and vegetable shop? Micky (a mutual friend) says this possession-obsession happens to people in their thirties. He says that's when life and relationships are like musical chairs: the music stops, and you just grab whatever's closest.

Well I don't care, I'm tired of being understanding. I'm tired of cheering up Iphigenia (not her real name). I've given her presents, I've taken her drinking, I've eaten buckets of ice-cream and watched thousands of videos and listened to soppy CDs. I close my eyes to sleep at night and all I see is an endless tacky movie starring Meg Ryan with a soundtrack by Celine Dion.

I've tried giving her hope. I've tried giving her hope-lessness. I've even tried saying I hate Pericles (not his real name). I've said that I find him moronic and gauche, because normally when you say something like that about a girlfriend's ex they're guaranteed to get back together.

But still her heart is broken. I've tried distracting her, finding other boys for her, telling her to concentrate on her career, but she persists in her repetitive lamentations.

Anyway, enough is enough; my life is starting to look like a very dark, short tunnel, so I've decided to force them back together. I've spread rumours, I've spread lies, I've arranged chance meetings, notes and flowers. I even went to a relationship counsellor on their behalf, during which time I gave both sides of their stories and asked how we could possibly work it out.

Finally, I resorted to an African spell. It required a lot of bizarre implements, but I found them all at Ikea. I made the effigies, I sang the chant, I burned the incense, I spent a fortune, I did the dance for forty-three hours, and now I'm waiting to hear if the spell's been successful.

The phone rings. 'Hi, it's me. I'm just ringing to tell you I'm completely over Pericles 'cause I've fallen in love with Ivan. Are you free for coffee? I'll come right over because I'm dying to tell you all about it!'

I hang up. That was Iphigenia. Oh, and by the way, Iphigenia is her real name.

heave-ho

It's the usual domestic scenario, just like a scene from *The Waltons*. The phone's ringing, the dinner's burning, the TV news is blaring, Epiphany is performing the Haka in the living room wearing a tutu and one of my bras, and I'm testing Zeke on his spelling:

'Spell "when".'

'W-E-N.'

'No.'

'Yeah, it's W-E-N.'

'No it's not, it's W-H-E-N.'

'Oh that "when", I thought you meant the other one.'

We finish the homework. I try to teach the kids to stare me in the eyes and say: 'My God, but you're lovely', but they insist on 'My God, but you're ugly'. I then announce it's time for sleep and Eppie tells me she feels sick. I immediately assume she's trying to worm her way into my bed (God knows why, because I can assure you nothing fabulous goes on there). So I ask her exactly where she's ill. 'Um, in my stomach, my head, my legs and my neck.' 'Oh,' I say, 'so your knees and elbows are alright then.' We laugh and I bounce her up and down on my knees until I put my back out.

The following morning Eppie eats a hearty breakfast and it's not until we're ready to leave for school and Zeke is attempting to bounce a football on her head as she tries to hit him with a broom that she again announces that she feels sick. I choose to ignore her. Although I'm reminded of something Tom Waites once said: 'On my gravestone I want it to say, I told you I was sick.'

You just can't tell if a child is telling the truth. Take buying shoes, for example. Children will always tell you the ones that you like (because they're cheap and functional) do not fit their feet. And the only ones that don't painfully cripple their toes to the point of permanent disfigurement are the $150 Nikes. See the kids walk victoriously out that shop door clad in the brand new footwear, then wait a couple of days and you'll see them wearing their old shoes again because the new ones 'just don't fit'.

So, pardon my scepticism, but I want my own lie detector. Of course I don't want Eppie to go to school and give some vile disease to her classmates, but I also don't want to teach her at the age of six to be an outright bludger . . . What next, a job as a government consultant?

I tried to think what tricks I would have played, but the last thing I wanted to do as a child was stay at home sick. I wasn't allowed to watch TV, and I had to stay in bed, entertained by the only precious article my family possessed: a one-armed, one-legged ceramic doll Mum had when she was a kid. There's only so much fun you can have with a toy you're not allowed to touch. One day sick in my family home and you'd lose your will to live.

So I don't really know the lengths people will go to to throw a sickie. Of course I've seen *Papillon* and remember when Dustin Hoffman's mate carved open his own leg, but this is actually the sort of thing Eppie would do. This is the girl who cut her foot on glass only last week and took the glass, the blood swab and the skin flap to school for Show and Tell.

Honestly, what hope have I of determining the truth from a six-year-old with a will of iron and an acting ability that drives her brother so completely mad that he's asked if he can divorce her?

I apply the usual tests. Have you done all your home-work? Are you happy with your friends? Is there some-thing about your hair you'd like to change? And Eppie replies 'No' to all of the above and insists she's just too sick to go to school. Well, Eppie you go to school and if you start to feel sick, go to the office and I'll come and get you. No, she persists, I'm just too sick and I have to stay at home. Buzzzzzz. She fails the test. We have a rule in our family that if you've got enough energy to fight about not going to school then you're well enough to go.

So she goes to school, with my phone number, and I hear nothing all day. I feel vindicated, I feel intuitive, I feel in control. 3.30, I see Eppie in the playground, I call her name, she comes running to her Mummy, the picture of health, she gives me a cuddle and a great big kiss, and then vomits all over my shoes.

secret men's business

It all started when I decided to get rid of the Barina. The rego was up, the bumper bar was in the boot, the car needed major Melanie Griffiths-zoosh surgery, so replacing it was a simple idea . . . which has ruined my life and destroyed my faith in humankind.

The last time I got rid of a car, I was eighteen and swapping a 21-year-old 'V-dub' for a couch. This time, I got rid of the Barina by exchanging it for a bar tab. So yes, I gave the Barina to a 35-year-old piss pot, who wanted to give it to her boyfriend for his twenty-first. Then Piss pot spent $550 getting the Barina ready for rego, collected it after two weeks at the mechanics, and, that night, the Barina was stolen and the following morning found wrapped around a tree. A tow truck charged $120 to cart the car back to PP's place, and now the unregistered Barina is parked in her treasured inner-city parking space while her own car braves the on-street parking where, only yesterday, someone side-swiped her vehicle causing $4758 damage.

But, anyway, back to *moi*. So I gave the Barina away and borrowed a friend's Audi. In the space of one week, I was driven into twice. Having decided that Audi is German for 'hit me', I took the car to the local smash repairer to get a quote and reversed it straight into a pole. The guy wanted cash payment for the quotes, I refused to pay, went without the quotes, and was chased aggressively up the road. Now there's another Sydney street I can no longer drive down, and I didn't even have a relationship with this bloke.

After the Audi, I cabbed it. During this time, I was hounded, bullied and tormented – and that was just listening to Alan Jones. I was sexually harassed, ripped off, and finally hugged by a white-glove-wearing Maori, who confided that he attends special clubs when he has those 'private yearnings'. 'Oh really, what clubs?' I asked understandingly. 'The AJC and Rotary,' he said.

I hired a car for the next seven days and, without a resident parking sticker, received $472 in parking fines. But it wasn't until I borrowed my lawyer's Saab for the day and he made me sign a contract, that I realised it was time to get my own car. I wanted a ute, but we had no use for the ute part so thought of accessorising with a kelpie. I thought of a Volvo, but you don't want to provide incentives for people to hit you, and I looked at a sports car, but they're all two-seaters and you just can't get roof-racks that firmly fasten kids.

Finally, I thought I'd ask a professional: 'I want something small, reliable and economical for about $15,000.' 'Oh, I've got just the thing, it's $23,750.'

At a dinner party, a used-car salesman mate-of-a-mate (who calls me half-a-mate) tried to sell me his girlfriend's car for $15,000 just after she'd told me it was worth $8000. However, the best offer was a car that had only done 70,000 kilometres – but the odometer had been broken since 1987.

I've test-driven fourteen cars and had each one checked out by George the Mechanic. After two months, I decided

on an old Merc and mentioned it at a tennis game where-
upon a stranger told me he knew the car and I was being
ripped off. (He's apparently best friends with the Merc
salesman and says I shouldn't trust him.) In tears, I took the
car to George and he told me it was fine. Relieved, I told a
friend, 'Thank God I can trust George.' 'I wouldn't,' she
replied, 'he ripped me off severely.'

In the meantime, I found a finance company, we agreed
on an interest rate, I went to sign the documents, and
found the interest rate was 2 per cent higher. I asked the
secretary why this was so and she said she didn't know, her
boss was playing golf, and, in just two hours, she was leaving this job and couldn't care two hoots.

Then, today, I received an anonymous call – 'You know,
you're making a huge mistake' – and I don't think it was a
comment on my lippie. Confused, I prayed for a sign while
bussing to work and saw a bug that looked like me splatter
on the windscreen. So I've decided to give up my job and
spend the rest of my life walking the kids to their engage-
ments. Yes, I'm going to get a little fresh air, 'cause I'm feeling rather carsick.

economy class

I'm in the plane; I've been here for eight hours. I'm on my way to Jakarta but we're going via Melbourne, Paris, Reykjavík, Lima, Calcutta and Hué. It's one of those budget tickets where you pay less in monetary terms but you forfeit several years of your life. I guess the bright side of it is I get an around-the-world ticket for the price of what should be a seven-hour flight.

I shift my feet from under my armpits to up my nose. There, that's more comfortable. I wonder who designed Economy Class – obviously people who work for the airline and know that they'll only ever be flying First Class. Personally I baulk at paying twice the price for nine inches more leg room and cutlery that won't snap. In fact the only seating arrangement I'd pay that much more for would be inside that little black box – at least if there's a crash you know you'll survive, and it couldn't be more uncomfortable than this.

I look out the window hoping to see some UFOs, but I really doubt I'll find any because all the aliens are in the plane with me.

It hasn't always been like this. During the first few stopovers all the passengers chatted amiably, but now we don't, because we hate each other. There's the man who farts. There's the extended family all playing full volume Nintendo, and there's the woman whose hairdo's so huge she prevents rows 30 through 61 from seeing the movie screen. No big loss, the featured movies are *Absolute Power*, a film about the sexual assault of a woman and her subsequent murder (my, how appropriate for all those kiddies in the audience) and *The Rock* (presumably a documentary about Sylvester Stallone's acting career).

As an intellectual exercise, I imagine the plane plummeting into the sea and floating to a desert island. I'm pondering who I would save and who I would eat. I decide I'd probably have to kill myself 'cause either way I don't think I could stomach these people.

If there were to be a crash I wouldn't have a clue what to do. Of course I've seen the safety performance many times, but I never concentrate. I always figure someone else will pay attention and I'll copy out their notes later. (My daughter, however, has read the safety card and asks if we can please crash into water because she wants to go down the slippery dip.)

Actually I think I'm better off not knowing what to do. I mean, considering these people can't get an overhead locker to stay shut, I can't imagine how in an emergency they can get hundreds of yellow pieces of plastic to fall spontaneously from the ceiling and provide oxygen. Really, has anyone ever seen one of those face masks? I don't believe they exist, and if they do I doubt it's oxygen they should supply as we crash; what about laughing gas instead.

And while we're on the subject, has anyone ever seen a life jacket under their seat? If so, you'll realise they're made out of the same material as floaties . . . which, by the way, have printed all over them in enormous letters: 'Not to be used as a flotation device'.

It seems to me reasonably obvious that airlines don't take this survival thing very seriously. Surely if they were really serious about it, they wouldn't attach a plastic whistle to your life jacket to attract attention, they'd give you a mobile phone.

The food arrives and the steward points to two identical mashed, beige meals and asks if I'd prefer beef or chicken. (Gee, those people in airline catering must have a fabulous sense of humour.) Despite its repulsive appearance, all the passengers settle down to eat the 'food' because, hey, we've all been a little too regular for too long. Personally I'm glad for the distraction; one can easily while away an entire hour of the flight just trying to open the orange juice.

Eating finished, I settle down to read *The Horse Whisperer*. (Days later I retell the story to a close friend and she asks if the book comes with a sick bag.) Suddenly I feel a tremendous pain in my leg, stomach and head. I fear it's the food invading my system until a huge bottom fair whacks me in the face. Aha, I realise it's toiletman again, climbing over me to get to the loo. While he's gone I steal his magazine and come across an airline ad. It features a naked woman and the words 'fly your dreams'. What is this, an ad for the Mile High Club? I don't long for the naked lady, but could I have the bed she's lying on please?

help!

The kids are going to the farm overnight and I've asked them to pack their own bags. Zeke's packed nothing but two footballs, and Eppie's packed a toy phone and a fairy suit. Nana and Papa arrive, collect the kids, and leave. I do a jig of youthful release, tidy the house, read the papers, imagine all the fabulous things I will do with my freedom, and after twenty-seven glorious minutes, find myself completely and utterly bored.

I've always had a problem with boredom. I fear it, it eats at me; I run from it, I hide. When Eppie was four, we flew to Japan, stayed one night and then returned, just for something to do.

Bored, bored, bored, bored. When I was eleven, I suggested to Mum that maybe life was meant to be boring because how else could it climax with death. So I'm bored. I call a friend. Not home. I call another. Not home. I call some more, some more, some more, and absolutely no one is home. Finally, I ring Frances who's bound to be home because she's always dreadfully depressed. We talk for a while about how tragic her pathetic life is and that cheers me up immensely.

I bump into a neighbour. We discuss how complicated and stressful modern life has become, and how we should all dispose of our possessions and move to small tropical islands because people who live on small tropical islands don't have a care in the world (except for those people who are malnourished, war-torn, disease-ridden and poor).

I go to buy some milk. The man behind the counter is extremely boring. I wonder if his mother fell asleep giving birth to him.

I visit the newsagent. The lady there is a little down. She says she's been low since Diana died. 'First Diana, then Mother Teresa,' she said. 'All the good people seem to be dying . . . and I'm worried I'll be next.'

I can feel my spirit slipping into tracky-daks and Ugh boots. I need something to do for a thrill. In the old days we all used to drink too much, smoke too much, and take lots of drugs. Now I think I'll go do the laundry and not separate the colours from the whites.

I go to the bookshop. I want the self-help section but need assistance to find it. I'm carrying a pen and pad so I look like I'm doing some sort of research, as opposed to desperately searching for a life. I find a few motivational books, but I can't be bothered reading them. There are best-sellers here covering every possible permutation of agony, hope and desperation. I wonder whatever happened to a friend of mine's manuscript, 'I'm O.K., You're Completely Fucked'.

I find *Eeyore's Gloomy Little Instruction Book* and, after a quick browse, realise I am Eeyore. Unlike other instruction books that tell you to cheer up by 'treating yourself to a cappuccino with extra froth', this one doesn't feign optimism. 'Having your missing tail recovered is all well and good, but remember that it will have to be re-attached. With a hammer and nail.'

I decide my life is completely pathetic and I don't know how I could have ever thought it was interesting. I wonder if I should get passionate about something, perhaps start collecting exotic ceramic frogs.

I need some goals. I decide to write a Do List in my Do List Book. I write down all the things I want to do, be and feel: go away more often; learn to cook; do a painting course. Today's Do List is identical to my last Do List, which is, sadly, identical to the one before that. What on earth am I doing with my life?

I'm bored; I'm becoming boring. I wonder if I should go and buy something amazing that makes me look intriguing. I'm thinking in terms of shaving my head or perhaps wearing a hat that says 'I'm funky' – but then I remember something I think Miss Piggy once said, 'Never wear a hat that's got more personality than you.'

I'm sinking low, I'm that soggy squishy mush of soap remaining in the soap dish. I look through old photo albums to try to remember what I looked like when I was happy. I'm hoping to bump into someone who'll introduce me to someone else, that way I'll know who I am.

Nothing to do, nowhere to go. It's at this point that I decide I should probably just sit down and write, because if I manage to write something that's completely self-obsessed and humourless I might even win an award.

gift of the fab

I'm in the queue at the supermarket. It's peak hour so the managers have sent half the cashiers off to lunch. I settle in for the duration, pinch a Freddo and grab a few mags from the rack. Read the goss, read the stars, read how to make valuable Christmas presents by weaving hats out of old plastic bags, then suddenly I'm served and back out on the street. It's raining so I hail a cab. One pulls over, I hop in and it's double-booked with my new best friend.

'Hello, I'm Sara, as in tiara, and you've got the same beautiful eyes as our family dog.'

'Thanks.'

'Well actually, I've just had him put to sleep.'

'Oh I'm sorry.'

'No don't be, we only got him because he matched the sofa. Yes, and then we got a new sofa . . . and, you know, common story. But let's face it, he was going to go to heaven one day, so basically he just caught an earlier bus. What's your name? Our dog's name was Pierce and he was a labrador. We called him after our family goldfish which died in a freakish antique-venetian-glass-chandelier-falling-from-the-ceiling-into-the-fishbowl incident. We were going to call him Stabbed In The Back, but we didn't want people to get the labrador confused with my father's last business partner.

'What we should have got was a schnauzer because they don't moult, or a maltese terrier because when they're asleep you can put them in the hall and they double up as a small flokati rug. Flokati rugs are coming back you know. Labradors are not.

'I haven't told the kids that Pierce has been put down but I have bought them each a lovely new outfit, so hopefully they won't notice he's missing. When Grandma died they each got a pony and neither of them has mentioned Grandma since. (It's not the first time we've put a pet to sleep. When the twins were born we put down all three of our brand-new kittens because people thought they were cuter than the kids.)

'You really should meet the twins, there's a boy called Pride and a girl called Prejudice. They're brilliant and beautiful and comparatively stable – all of which I put down to the fact that I had a very natural birth. It was in the Range Rover at the hospital car park with a gyno who was wearing R. M. Williams riding boots.

'I wish this cab was a huge four-wheel drive because they're so much safer, you know – though not for the car you hit, of course. But they're so big and difficult to park that the chances are pretty high that you will hit someone one day, so it's good to know that you'll be safe when you do . . . and that you can listen to random-select from ten different CDs while you're waiting for the ambulance to arrive for your victim.

'Oh, here's our stop. Our house is called Wuddamunja. It's Aboriginal for "Our Home". Well, their home really, but it's our home now. Ours is the Tuscan villa in the middle, in between the Tuscan villa on the left and the Tuscan villa on the right. Everyone in our suburb just loves Tuscany, and that's where Bernard and I want to live for twelve months. We did want to live in Provence for a year, but someone's already done it. We've done the interior *à la* English country cottage. Do you know why? Because I'm a classicist and individuality may come and it may go but Liberty Print obviously will always remain.

'Oh look, there's Bernard. I know he looks gay but believe me he's not. He's really very heterosexual, despite the fact that he dresses so well. Anyway, drop in, but if someone who doesn't look like me answers the door then that'll probably be me. I'm having my face done early next Tuesday, and then I'm going into therapy to find the real me.

'Next year I'm having my breasts done, but Bernard can claim that op. as a tax deduction because my breasts help with his business. I'm actually a director of a lot of Bernard's companies. It's a tremendous responsibility to carry – you know, not knowing what we'll do next, not knowing what we're doing now, not knowing what we've ever done, and receiving a huge non-existent income for my input-output thingy.

'So, do, do drop round – it's been delightful chatting – but when you come over would you mind wearing dark glasses, I don't want the children seeing your eyes and being reminded of the dog.

'Ciao.'

pot head

My fifty-year-old cleaner arrived late the other morning.
(There, it's out; yes I have a cleaner, God forgive me, I'm not
a superwoman but, take note, she's not a very good
cleaner.) Anyway, like all good guilt-ridden daughters of
housework-frayed mothers, I'd gotten up early to clean my
house before the cleaner came. I'd made the lunches, ironed
the uniforms, done the hair, force-fed the breakfasts,
dressed the kids, and was ready to leave. Well, we waited
and waited and waited and waited until finally the cleaner
waltzed in and giggled: 'I've just had the most enormous
spliff and I'm really, really stoned.'

I think I got spoilt by domestic help in Bali. Yes, I
enjoyed the sun, the sea, the blah blah blah, but more than
anything else, I enjoyed, no, found fabulous, no, became
compulsively, obsessively addicted to having people at my
beck and call, obeying my every whim. In just six days I
learnt to see the world from the perspective of one of my
kids.

Finding Domestic Help Bliss is like buying your first
fitted bra, hailing a cab driver who's heard of your destination, or discovering a pain killer that really works. Two
men, two women, working shifts, doing nothing unless I
ordered it. In the end, I found myself searching for jobs to

keep them busy and saying things to the kids like: 'Go outside and play in the dirt and then come and walk through the house.'

I've always been shocking at getting help around the house. Like most women I'm too generous, too understanding, and absolutely begging to be fleeced. Who can forget the builder who came to construct a garden wall, charged three times his quote, took two years to complete the job and, on the very last day, reversed his truck into the new wall and then tried to sue me for damages? Or the live-in babysitter who was so thick I used to pay for her to take little day trips just so she'd be safely away from the kids?

Or what about the cleaner with 'difficulties at home' who used to sit at my kitchen table sobbing into her hanky while I cleaned the house myself for three hours and then paid her 45 bucks (actually I often paid her 50 because I felt too stingy asking for change).

Thanks a lot, Women's Lib. In the old days I would have raised the kids, done the cooking-shopping-cleaning bumpf, and gone stark, raving mad. Now I do all that *and* go to work and *still* go stark raving mad. At least in those days they had the luxury of popping Valium, but who's got time for that?

Of course, I try to think of timesavers, for example wearing Velcro on the soles of my shoes so I can collect the lint balls from the carpet while I dust, but it's difficult to motivate oneself towards project time management when you think the project is a waste of time anyway. 'What's the point in ironing?' I have been heard to say. 'As soon as you've done it it's wrinkly again.' (A theory which, may I point out, can also be applied to sex.)

My preferred option would be to leave the housework untouched and undone until the kids are grown. I've tried roping the children in to do their share, but they won't have a bar of it. 'Zeke, it's your responsibility to clean up the mess because you made the mess in the first place.' 'No Mum, actually the mess is your responsibility, because you're the one who wants it tidied up.'

What a conundrum: working woman, feral children, two hands, twenty-four hours, selfish need to sleep occasionally. I need an assistant. I need a slave. Basically, I need a wife.

Actually I'd prefer to have a man about the house, but I'm sure that if I ever found a man who was at all capable of doing anything useful I would immediately find him tremendously attractive and end up in a relationship. At which point he would stop doing things around the house and I'd end up waiting on him.

And besides, I don't need a bloke all the time, I just think sometimes it would be nice. He could deal with the car mechanic and get called 'sweetheart', he could talk to the bank that said a loan would be easier if I went and got married, or the man at customs who took me aside because I 'looked suspicious travelling alone with two kids', or even the prominent life insurance company which wanted to charge me a 50 per cent loading because of the dangerous nature of my work. 'But I'm a writer and I sit at my desk and my desk is not on a fault line.' 'No, that's not what we have a problem with,' he said. 'It's the single mother bit.'

Actually, according to all the information I can glean on this issue, I don't need a bloke at all, I just need different products. Oh yes, apparently I'm using the wrong face cream. I've got to find out what hosiery, snail killer, margarine and other products those perfect women use and then really lash out on them.

Meanwhile, I pop home to pay the cleaning lady. The house hasn't been touched. I ask if she's done the cleaning and she says yes, she was very thorough, and presents me with one extremely bright and shiny pot. She holds it in awe and then says with pride: 'And if you look underneath, you can see your face.' Fabulous, maybe I just need what she uses.

no man is an island

but lots of people are pigs

Moët poet

i have,
decided,
to become,
a poet.

I have no talent but I don't think that will matter. Only last week I became the *nouvelle enfant terrible* of the visual arts scene by submitting a plain, blank primed canvas to the Museum of Contemporary Art and signing it while naked in the gallery cafeteria. I was confronting, shocking and very, very popular. But I've conquered that scene now. I'm moving on to be a poet. Gore Vidal once said having no talent is no longer enough. But I think we all know he was wrong.

I first thought of becoming a poet after being inspired by Hilga Rortland and her extraordinary poem,

We had a love
unique, to us
but same.
Turtle he was
and yet, to me
my one.

Last would it
until the truck
came, squish.

Now sure, something may have been lost in translation from the Dutch (a language which abounds in poignancy and humour), but the poem still stands straight and proud as being absolutely brilliant. I personally hope Hilga has written something similar about dairy products because as G. K. Chesterton once pointed out: 'Poets have been mysteriously silent on the subject of cheese.'

Hilga has inspired my greatest work to date, a poem entitled 'Kettle'.

Kettle,/ vessel of liquid,/ servicing the pot,/ used,
are you man or are you woman,
what is that scream you make?

Modern poets find beauty in meaningless simple things that you and I might previously have thought of as meaningless simple things, for example: *Dust./ Are you Happy?* or, *Carrot./ Were you my mum?*

Many people, of course, are blind to the real value of modern poetry, preferring the more classic style of Keats, Shelley and Coleridge. But as far as I'm concerned, Spring and the burning deck have been done, and rhyming is out, I shout. Of course one can blithely say that contemporary poetry is no more complex than a child's playground rhyme, but can one really compare *'I turned to see my shoe step, oh step, upon the ground, ground, ground'* with *'What's the time, half past nine, hang your bosoms on the line, if they burst, I don't care, go and buy another pair'*? (Now guess which is the playground rhyme?) Besides, it's easy to criticise, isn't it? Antoine De Rivarol once reviewed a two-line poem with 'Very nice, though there are dull stretches.'

Of course, not all contemporary poetry is brilliant. *'My heart, bleeds like pain upon the snow'* is not fabulous, but *bleeds like/ pain/ my heart/ upon the snow* most definitely is.

Modern poetry is all about spacing, punctuation and maintenance of the lower case. And if you want to do it properly, you must observe these rules. One must also read up on how-to poetry books. (Like Mariah Carey, one can never have too much.) My favourite was *Getting Inside the Writer's Mind — What Do Writers Really Think About?* and, after completing it, I immediately wrote 'Me Moi Io'.

I find writing poetry enormously fulfilling and, as I leather-thong through life, I can barely restrain my creative urges (*Weather report with thy sadistic promises — as I turn you on, do you do the same for me*). Oops, there goes another one. But the problem is contemporary poets make very little money. One could suggest there are fundamental economic reasons for this, to do with supply and demand, but let's follow a different path, for surely there must be a poetic lane that leads to enormous wealth. Ah yes, the western Haiku, or advertising slogan: *Life's short play hard* — Reebok; and Nike — *Just do it*. Or the National Bank's simply inimitable *Never lose sight of what you set out to achieve*. (No matter what new and exciting charges you may incur.)

Yes, I think I will pursue advertising next. Be gone,

macraméd poncho. Of course, embracing the dollar will have me expelled from my poetry club, but just imagine what the socio-political intrigue will do for the value of my paintings! I can feel a slogan coming on now. It's a slogan-slash-poem about the essence of womanhood, about truth, restraint and passion. It's for a brand new fragrance called 'Obsession': *Be careful, or you'll use it all up in one go.*

flops

Some people can type and some people jist cont. Some people can long jump four times their height. Some people resolve conflict between warring nations. Some people find cures for horrendous diseases. Some people nurture the poor, the sick and the needy. And some people are rich and famous, idolised and adored, even though they appear to have no talent, craft or even personality. These people are called 'movie stars', and I want to be one of them. In fact, I want to be Alice Twinkle.

Alice is the woman that females want to be and males want to have. This is because she possesses what we in the trade refer to as the indefinable (not to be confused with the non-existent). I won't go on about the indefinable, because of course I can't, so instead I shall talk about Alice's breasts.

Alice's breasts are not like Pamela's breasts, although the four are related. Alice's breasts signify Alice's sense of irony and razor wit and are not, as some would have you believe, the only thing that stands out about her. The Human Bra, sorry, I mean Alice, is obviously a very talented, beautiful, intelligent woman. I first came across Alice in a short film she did called *Has Anyone Seen The Other Half Of My Dress?* (Which was, of course followed by the Liz Hurley sequel, *Oi, Here It Is*.)

Though some have criticised Alice's more recent acting

forays as being like 'watching a dead snail go even deader', there is a reason for this temporary lull in her dramatic development, and that reason is Alice's breasts. Don't tell a soul, but Alice's breasts aren't real. She's had enormous breasts implanted, and now a lot of the time and effort that used to be spent on honing her acting craft is used to help her stand upright. And I think we all agree, she does stand upright very well. She also sits down very well, and grows her hair quickly.

(May I point out at this juncture that Alice is a goer and a tryer and that's why we love her, and I for one am proud of the fact that a momentary inability to act, or 'actor's block' as we call it, has not prevented Alice from continuing to appear in innumerable international high-budget films. She is a truly brave and inspiring woman.)

Other things that have helped make Alice the phenomenon that she is include . . . actually, just back to the breasts for the moment. I think they show that Alice must have a very strong back, and everybody likes a strong woman. In fact being a strong woman is the theme of Alice's new war movie. Although frequently referred to as 'a workout video in army fatigues', this film is in fact at the forefront of an exciting new cinematic genre which replaces dialogue with grunts. Furthermore, the film exquisitely focuses upon Alice's natural skills and avoids revealing any small inabilities she may possess. This is why Alice's part is pretty well a non-speaking role, but her right nipple is featured in the film's poster.

Not everyone would let themselves be upstaged by their nipple (assuming it *is* her nipple and not a nipple double), but Alice is really a very generous person. Alice's breasts have often hogged Alice's limelight, but Alice has never complained. Indeed, so prominent are they within her more recent works that many are suggesting Alice's breasts may soon be headlining the credits, above Alice's own name.

Rumour also has it that Alice's breasts are possibly forming their own production company. God help us if they produce flops.

But enough of Alice's breasts.

Breasts, sorry, I mean Alice, is obviously very smart and very confident because you would have to very smart and very confident to allow people to think you were just a pair of hooters. And everybody loves a strong, generous, smart and confident woman. Alice's breasts not only tell us all this about her, but also that Alice is rich, because you need to be rich to have bosoms that big, since you need a spacious home to house them. (I am poor and live in a terrace and, while I would love two massive bazookas to rest my TV dinner on, there quite simply isn't the room in our house for myself, the two kids and two whopper boobs; not if we're planning on getting a domestic pet.)

Other things that help make Alice a phenomenon worth approximately $16 million per movie and the subject of 22,300 Internet sites, include the fact that she is a mother (and let's face it, someone becomes a mother only 1,326,689 times per minute across the globe), and the fact that despite paparazzi shots of her alleged cellulite Alice has managed to keep her marriage intact. The woman is a legend.

independently us

Every school morning we rush out the door and Eppie says, 'I forgot my news.' Then I reopen the house, she runs back inside and grabs the nearest thing for 'show and tell'. Today she took our metal egg basket, which is shaped like a chicken, and told the class it's Helen, her new pet. I heard of one little girl who told show and tell that daddy had hit mummy and the policeman came to visit.

Eppie always unlocks the car and Zeke always dives in the front seat first. They then fight over whose turn it is to sit next to Mum and I order them both into the back. We drive down the road quite sedately, but when we get to the intersection at the bottom of our street, where absolutely no one gives way, we barge across, with my hand on the horn, and the three of us yell at the oncoming cars, 'Watch out you silly bloody idiot.'

There's been a lot of talk lately about the detrimental effect divorce has on children, so I'm looking for signs of delinquency in my kids. They're argumentative, demanding, wilful and self-obsessed, but I understand this is completely normal. Once teenagers, however, my children are at risk of psychiatric problems, drug taking, promiscuity, and pathetic educational achievement. Sounds like my adolescence, except my parents weren't divorced.

It annoys me, all this research about the devastated children of the so-called 'broken home'. What a fabulously predictable backflip from earlier studies that claimed Australian children appear to adapt after divorce and are as emotionally whole as children whose families remain intact. It's all a little bit like the cyclical nature of fashion. As the miniskirt of the sixties returned, with hot pants and bell-bottoms hard on its heels, so too have we seen intellectual fads come and go and return.

So what's happened? Call me a cynic, but is it just possible that this new theory is merely the product of a group of intellectuals validating their tenure by producing a paper designed to create drama and distress? How sexy, how glamorous, how absolutely nineties to state that the indulgence of the parents hurts and scars the children. What a cracker of a scandalous idea. Heap the guilt upon the divorced because, yeah, they're just cop-outs anyway: self-indulgent, whimsical irresponsibles who choose to go through the trauma of divorce and subsequent impoverishment just because they got bored. Does anyone research the detrimental effects of couples staying together 'for the sake of the kids', and the huge burden that is for a child to bear? Hey, how about a survey titled 'Watching Your Parents Negate Their Lives: Damage to a Child's Heart and Mind'?

I may be wrong (I haven't slept for nine years), but I do know a lot of moneyed, middle-class, straight-teethed, nuclear-families' kids who grew up to be complete psychos. The sufferings children of divorced parents allegedly experience due to domestic aggression, financial strain, frustration and resentment, are all factors that can exist whether mum/dad is divorced, or married, or living as a chaste asparagus farmer in Putney.

So, don't brand my children the underclass because it makes you feel better about playing martyr to your relationship. And get off your bloody high horse. Don't you think we all hope to live happily ever after? Don't you think we all want love and comfort and security? Don't you think we all wish our husband didn't drink, or earned potloads of money, or the wife didn't go batty, and the kids all won scholarships to private schools, or that we could play tennis to relieve our stress, and have massages and manicures, and get socially sloshed on a bottle or two of posh plonk? Of course we do. So what is the point in all this research? To advise people that no matter what their circumstances they should remain with their partner (if you haven't been in a miserable marriage you can have no idea how naive and ludicrous that proposition is), or is it perhaps to tell us that only the financially secure, socially acceptable, non-changing elite should be trusted to have our children?

How can you tell what will last and what will not? A divorcing friend of mine mentioned the wife's dressage horse to his lawyer. 'What did you say – dressage horse? Well there you go, there's your problem right there. No marriage will ever survive with a partner who's into dressage.'

They're playing brandings now. Zeke is throwing the ball and Eppie is the target. The game will finish when one of them gets hurt, so I'm waiting on the sideline with my magic kisses.

Zeke asks Eppie for a bite of her banana. 'No,' she replies.

'Eppie,' I quickly interject, 'we are a sharing, caring family and we all respect one another. So what do you say when Zeke asks for a bite of your banana?'

'No, thank you.'

my favourite Martians

It's 7 a.m., I have an eight o'clock meeting. Son wakes up, calls me for a cuddle, looks me in the eye and softly whispers, 'You know, from the side you look just like Woody Allen.' ('I don't mean to upset you Mum, I'm just being pacific.')

I go to wake Daughter. I say through her bedroom door, 'Come on darling, time to get up', then I'm back downstairs to hurry Son. Is he clothed already, breakfasted too? No, he's riding his skateboard outside in the street wearing a towel over his pyjamas. Seven times I call him to come in and get dressed; on the last he says, 'What, I can't hear you?' I repeat my request – he says can't I have one more ride, I say no, he has one more ride, and then walks dog poo through the house.

I take the poisonous shoe upstairs to wash the poisonous poo off. On the way I open Daughter's door and say a little louder, 'Come on, it's time to get up.' I return downstairs with the shoe. Son's still not dressed nor breakfasted, and is playing tennis on the kitchen wall. It's 7.25. I tell him to stop, and he says, 'Mum wait, just watch this.' He hits the ball hard and high into the light, which crashes from the ceiling and shatters over the floor. He looks at me like it's all my fault because I'm the one who asked him to stop. 'Help me tidy up,' I say. 'I can't, I'm not wearing shoes.'

7.35 a.m. and Son has got himself sunblocked and

dressed in a desperate goody-goody catch-up. He's showing off, standing ready by the door when he remembers with horror he hasn't finished his school journal, *What I Did On The Weekend*. We hurriedly yell what we did on the weekend and realise it's exactly the same as his entry from last week, and the week before. Pride cometh quickly; we need colour, we need movement, we need to plagiarise someone else's life. (I bumped into a car at the ABC car park recently and it took me seventeen drafts to leave a note that finally read: 'Please ring regarding your car.')

It's 7.40. I call to Daughter from downstairs, 'Hurry up, it's nearly time to go.' There's no reply, so I call more loudly. 'We're leaving in five minutes.' Still no response, so I climb half the stairs. 'If you don't come downstairs this instant, I, oh what's the point . . .' I carry Daughter to the shower. The water's too hot, then it's too cold, then, of course, the water's too wet.

I return to journal-writing Son to witness him spilling a glass of milk down the front of his shirt. I go upstairs to find another and discover Daughter lying in my bed. I ask her why and she replies, 'Because I love you so much.' Son calls for his shirt. I run downstairs. Naked Daughter follows me and proceeds to dance in front of the mirror. 'What are you doing?' I ask, a tad annoyed. 'I'm drying myself, of course.'

I send her away to get dressed immediately and she returns wearing a hat. 'Where's the rest of your uniform?' 'I can't find it,' she says. 'Well it's on the couch as usual.' And sure enough that's where it is – and Son is sitting on it. I iron the kit and kaboodle again and say, 'Sit down and eat your Weet-Bix.' 'I don't like Weet-Bix.' 'Yes you do, you've eaten them for years, you love them.' 'No, I don't, I hate Weet-Bix, I just forgot to tell you.'

I prepare toast and a banana for Daughter while Daughter draws Texta all over her arms. I send her upstairs to wash. Son trips her, Daughter cries, Son replies it's not his fault, she's the one who tripped over his foot. I ask Son to tidy up but he knocks over my coffee instead. Son mops the floor with Daughter's newly ironed shirt, gets up, hits his head and begins to cry. Daughter laughs, Son calls her a 'boozie head', Daughter starts to cry. Send Daughter upstairs for a new shirt then find her in her closet writing pop song 'Oi Oi Boys, We Love You' . . . This reminds Son he has a class talent quest and hasn't prepared a zot. 'We were going to do a thing about Mariah Carey but Jack lost her voice.' I dress him in a red velvet dressing gown, raise the collar, and tell him he's a vampire. He says he looks like a stupid girl. (But he actually looks more like Liberace.)

We get in the car, Son's forgotten his school bag and Daughter's forgotten her lunch. They run back to the house in a flurry and twirl, and I see Daughter's also forgotten her undies.

Back in the car, ready for school with 30 seconds up my sleeve. I ask Son what he wrote in his journal. 'Oh, I said that on the weekend I went off to Mars.' 'What?' shrieks Daughter, on hearing this. 'How come on the weekend he went to Mars and we didn't!'

'Actually, Eppie, if the truth be known, we go to Mars every morning.'

dear me

According to the women's mags, within the same week Nicole Kidman, Dannii Minogue and Fergie all declared an overwhelming desire to swim in the sea with killer sharks. This news obviously prompts the question – are these women not getting enough good sex or do they just need my advice?

The following is a limp adaptation of an advice book I wrote several years ago, which can now be found in remainder bins throughout the best bargain bookstores of Australia. (They offered to sell them to me at $1.50 a copy but even I didn't want them.) I resurrect it because my instincts tell me the world's ready for it (mind you, my instincts also told me to wear such a hat to the Melbourne Cup that complete strangers called at me from the stalls, 'Hey, who's the park ranger?'). Anyway, here we go (music up and under).

No man is an island, but lots of people are pigs. Avoid those who are selfish, stupid, greedy or conceited, and then try not to get lonely. Do not confuse vanity with pride or self-esteem. Do not be obsessed about your weight. If you really want to make your bum look smaller, extend the crack with an eyebrow pencil.

Learn to spell and learn to count, but all the maths you

need to know you've probably learned by the age of seven. Do not waste time, do not stuff your bikini bra with anything soluble, do not volunteer as the target for brandings. Laugh. Join a club. Play a sport.

Love. Recognise when a relationship has turned to compromise, and when foreplay is just stage one rapid eye movement. Avoid lovers in Cuban heels, men with party tricks, and women who say 'no-one understands me'.

Try hard to be optimistic, energetic and enthusiastic; enthusiasm alone is not enough (a hard lesson I learned as a teenager willing my breasts to grow). Do not wear long socks with sandals. Tell the school when your child has head lice. Empty your vacuum cleaner, wash your car, defrost your fridge, give old clothes to the needy. Spring clean your acquaintances.

Be open, be honest, do not be too proud. Listen. Understand when you're being boring. Learn from the experience of others, but never accept the advice of anyone who is either still wearing shoulder pads or likely to be dead before their advice is proved to be wrong. Remember, true wisdom only really comes when your breasts are the past tense of pert.

Be generous, but do not try to impress. Be aware that the best thing to give someone who has everything is always absolutely nothing. Do not be greedy, nor acquisitive; give to charity and file the receipt.

Avoid users. When the going gets tough the tough get going, and the weak will bludge a lift. Do not sit on heaters. Avoid crossing your legs. Fight for yourself. Hug. Believe in something but always check your change.

Work hard, play hard, live by sports-shoe slogans. Tell the truth whenever possible and always remember your lies. Try to start either a political movement or a religion that respects and worships bikini-line hair.

Check your oil, sing loudly in the car, speak in silly voices. Think before you talk. (You will always start everything off on the wrong foot if the other one is stuck in your mouth.)

Do not suffer in silence. Do not read your stars. Do not feel sad when you're not invited somewhere, have your own party; perhaps put cream on your feet. Take control. Compliment people; it puts them off their guard. Save time, judge books by their covers. Remember, there are video cameras in almost every lift.

Know your own power, do not snore during sex, do not confuse yourself with anyone from *Melrose Place*. Be brave in love, career, friendship and facial electrolysis. Watch your diet and live by the motto *carpe diem*: a fish a day.

Make friends, socialise, have dinner parties. Try to find a partner who respects and adores you. And always remember you will never be number one in the life of a man who has a nickname for his willy.

Marry people who laugh at your jokes. Do not use spray deodorant with your mouth open. Wash up at the end of the meal, not at the end of the week. Hire a cleaner, do not befriend him or her. Check the levels in your grog bottles and count your CDs. Remember one day cellulite will be fashionable.

Do not envy the lives of others and, remember, no matter how much you wish it to be true, attractive, intelligent, successful people are not necessarily miserable. (Although people with pert, fat-free bottoms do suffer when they attend community theatre.)

Organise. Have goals and try to achieve them. Do not whip yourself. Plan to write a best-selling autobiography when you're old, then claim your whole life as a tax deduction.

Sometimes life is hard, sometimes life's too easy. Life is a near-death experience. The meaning of life is . . .

(The above advice is soon to be released as a blockbuster CD, major motion picture, and possibly a lipstick range.)

party pooper

It's 10.30 p.m. The party started at 8 and I'm standing outside the front door with Nigel. Nigel is my handbag, quite literally, as in his pockets are my Ventolin, lipstick, comb, purse and keys. The subsequent bulge has ruined the fall of his trousers, but I've told Nigel it's very flattering.

We're late. Not fashionably. Not frantically. Not excitingly. Just late. Actually that's not true. We are calculatingly, determinedly, deliberately late because I don't want to go to this party. I'm not moody, sick, tired or hormonal, and I'm having a reasonably good hair night. So why don't I want to go to this party? Well, because I don't actually know the woman who's invited me, and I think she thinks I'm her best friend.

It all started a year-and-a-half ago. I was in the supermarket, thought she was someone else and waved hello down the aisle. A couple of weeks later she saw me in a coffee shop, recognised me from The Aisle Nine Incident and waved hello from the door. I responded with an Oh-hi-you're-the-person-I-confused-with-someone-else-aren't-I-silly sort of wave, then a month after that I saw her in the newsagency and she said 'Hi, how are you?' Then six weeks later I saw her in the park and we had such a friendly 'How's everything going? Fine, what about you?'

chat that I started to wonder if indeed maybe she *is* the friend I originally mistook her for – and if I have in fact mistaken her for herself.

This behaviour continued unclarified for the rest of the year, and then last Christmas she gave me a Christmas card (name completely illegible). Well, I of course felt guilty receiving her card and responded a week later by giving one to her, but not wanting to make it obvious that I'd only organised mine after receiving hers, I wrote in red crayon in the front left-hand corner of the envelope: 'Held at the post office.'

And then this Christmas she invited me to her party and I couldn't say 'no' because when someone asks you three months in advance 'Are you doing anything on the 18th of December?' you can hardly say 'Yes, I am.' They might be inviting you to their wedding, or to Pavarotti in the Park, or on a blind date with some jetsetting, though well-grounded, extraordinarily gorgeous, successful, under-standing and love-needing, perfect-match bloke. So you can't just say 'I'm busy.' Well, you can, but you don't, do you? No, you say 'I'm not sure, why?' And then before you know it they've said they're having a party and you have to say 'Oh great.' Then you spend the next three months thinking of ringing to say that you're terribly sorry but you didn't realise you'd be overseas and wondering if you should buy yourself a round-the-world ticket and spend the weekend of the party flying just to make sure that no one who knows you sees you at the fruit shop and dobs you in to the party giver.

But if you say yes, then you really must go, so Nigel and

I have a plan, and that is to arrive late, when everyone else is too pissed to talk but not so legless that they'll forget we did actually turn up. We'll do a circuit of the room, repeat a mantra of 'Hi, we must catch up', hug the hostess, say 'Don't you look fab', and then quietly slip out.

I can hear the music. Sounds like the party's happening. Perfectly planned, perfectly timed, we knock on the door . . . and it's opened to reveal a party consisting of seven bored strangers in limp conversation looking thrilled to bits that we have arrived. (If only my 'friend' hadn't opened the door we could have just yelled 'trick or treat' and run away.)

I tell Nigel to clutch his stomach and fall to the floor so I can call an ambulance and we can leave. He says 'Don't be ridiculous, get in there, make the most of it, you never know you might meet someone who'll change your life.' (Nigel has obviously seen someone whom he thinks will change his life, so I decide to wait until he's rejected and then continue with my plans.) I mingle while I wait. Three men discuss cars in the kitchen. Two women discuss relationships outside the toilet. A lonely man wanders the room lifting objects and studying them intently. I feel sorry for his amateur attempts to make himself seem aloof and charming when absolutely nothing he does could possibly counter-balance the fact that he's wearing grey zip-on vinyl shoes. (Whereas a man believes his car is his phallic extension, women in fact know it to be a man's shoes.)

Nigel returns. I tell him to go into the laundry with his mobile, ring the hostess and say there is a bomb in the building. He tells me to faint. I say why don't we have a lovers' tiff. And he says don't be silly they can tell that he's gay just by the way he dips his Jatz. The hostess comes up and says hello and Nigel and I say 'Great Party.'

An hour passes and we talk about the cheese balls. Then at 12 o'clock (the polite 'I've stayed long enough' hour), suddenly everyone says 'Lovely party' and disappears out the door. So Nigel and I catch the wave and say 'Thanks for the party we had a great time.' And she says 'What are you doing on the 27th of March?' and we say we don't know and she says 'Oh good, 'cause I'm having a party for my birthday.' We accept the invitation and crumble out the door. We'd better learn her name before we sing Happy Birthday. Partying is such sweet sorrow.

visible panty line

My resolutions are all broken. I've given up on trying to change myself for the better and have decided to criticise others. It's summer and everyone is having fun, except me, just lying here, thinking too much and trying to find some meaning for the forthcoming year of my life. I've toyed with tap dancing, Judaism, and a gluten-free diet, but at this point I'm pretty sure that I'll become a politician. My platform will be women's rights and my slogan will be Bring Back the Visible Panty Line (or Let's Ban Those Stupid G-strings).

Having spent five tortuous hours on a plane recently doing myself possibly irreparable damage with a G-string affected by the G-force, I would like to take this opportunity to launch an official comeback for the Visible Panty Line. The G-string is obviously a backlash against feminism, a mechanism of male sexual fantasy, either symbolic of bondage, or suggesting to males 'Oh my God she's wearing no undies – even less work for me.' The G-string is obvious sexual harassment, and the discarding of the VPL, and the subsequent adoption of the G-string, have led to grave problems in female development. No wonder we find it difficult to juggle children and a career, are moody and distant, and can't break through the glass ceiling. No wonder people say 'What's up her bum?' I'll tell you: it's a G-string.

If the bra strap, with or without hanky, can become fashionable again, if women can wear nothing but lingerie down catwalks and to cocktail parties, then I want to know why the VPL can not only return, but become its own fabulous fashion statement. I am woman, hear me roar, I'm wearing Cottontails and my bot's not sore.

Of course you don't need to get into politics to have a profound effect on the world; you can also die while faddishly famous, have breast implants that are bigger than your head, or have sex with Mick Jagger. But I want to go into politics for the perks and because I believe that, in the same way funerals make people laugh, parliament must be terribly funny (not that sex with Mick Jagger wouldn't be, of course).

I plan to get in quick at the next election by stealing promises from *Grimm's Fairy Tales* and offering my supporters scratch lottery tickets. I'll be attractive to men by wearing very short skirts, high heels and cleavage-hugging tops, and I'll be attractive to women by slagging off men who get turned on by women in short skirts, high heels and cleavage-hugging tops. So as not to appear threatening to either of the sexes I am going to get a dreadful perm. During the election process I will encourage allegations regarding my lurid past (working on the Jack Nicholson principle), and not apologise for any incidents (because it was apologising that almost ruined Hugh Grant's career). And then, once elected, I'm going to make passionate love trysts compulsory for all public figures, and make it illegal to hire mime artists for public outdoor celebrations.

I'll make busy mothers the ministers for each department. They'll determine national policies on the phone while ironing the school uniforms and preparing the school lunches. My mother will do the nation's budget.

I'll keep men in my government so they can lift heavy things. But I won't let them be involved in any substantial decision-making process unless they're dying of a terminal disease, because sadly this appears to be when most men find the real meaning of life.

Being predominantly women, my government will be pacifist (women would never resolve conflict with war, we'd just invite all our enemies over for dinner and then talk about them when they went to the toilet). We'll abandon the defence forces, and encourage the whole world to rent land in Australia so they've all got a reason to defend the place. I will ban private health insurance and negative gearing on residential investment properties. I will make casinos pay huge taxes on their profits and I'll force people in the money market to study an eastern religion. I'll make it illegal not to return phone calls, I'll make it punishable by imprisonment if your dog poos in the street, and I'll develop a special language for parents so they can talk behind their children's backs, right in front of their faces.

After a couple of years I'll retire to collect a huge super cheque and lifetime travel discounts, and set up my own international businesses utilising the powerful connections I've networked while leader of the nation (and only reappear on the political scene when it serves me well to put my two bob's worth in . . . sorry Bob).

A: Have you ever taken a serious political stand on anything?

B: Yes, for 24 hours I refused to eat grapes – *Sleeper*, Woody Allen.

No comment, but don't quote me – Dan Quayle.

dreading the wedding

I was thinking how a woman can carry a baby inside her for nine months and this is considered normal, while a man can float in a sailing race from Sydney to Hobart and be considered a legend, when suddenly the phone rang. It was Lola, an old school friend ringing to ask if I would please speak at her wedding. Having considered her impending wedding to be a joke from the start (he, a middle-aged and attituded consummate bore, and she, a high-achieving, beautiful success who could have been with someone who was at least a *Homo sapiens* had her loudly ticking clock not distracted her, removed any semblance of taste, and encouraged her to settle for a well-earning log), I found myself saying 'Yes'.

I've never spoken at a wedding but I've performed for audiences who yell 'show us ya tits' while hurling beer cans at my head and whose idea of intellectual conversation is a fart joke, so I figured this wedding gig would be easy. I saw myself telling a few affectionate rip-snorters at Lola's expense and being the hit of the show. 'Sure I'll speak at the reception,' I said. 'No, not at the reception,' she replied, 'as part of the actual ceremony.'

Oh fab, palpitations, no matter what your religion, age, sex, or height, you cannot tell dick jokes from the pulpit. You also can't really tell jokes about love or marriage, or mention the word divorce, which is, of course, like discussing Russian roulette and leaving the bit out about the bullet.

'Couldn't I speak after dinner?' 'No, Natalie's speaking then.' (Oh, an A-list friend.) 'And one of Jeremy's friends is reading at the wedding and I need you to read something too.' (Oh, so it's political then.) 'What's he reading?' 'Something from the Bible.' 'Well, what do you want me to read?' 'I don't care, just anything.' (Oh my, this is heartfelt, how about an excerpt from Daniel Thornton's *Hey, What Poop is That?*) 'What, anything?' 'Yes, anything, but remember no dick jokes.'

'Sorry Lola, me again, just thinking about this speak-at-your-wedding-thing, and I was wondering if you think you might cancel. It's just that it doesn't seem so long ago that you told me all men have the hearts and minds of small half-green potatoes.' 'Yes, well that was before I met Jeremy.' (No, actually it was a few months after.) 'You also said that promising to love someone for the rest of your life was like promising to eat nothing but red jubes until the day you die, you said marriage should be done retrospectively, when you've led your life lovingly together, and you said any decision-making while madly in love should be deemed invalid due to an altered state of consciousness and diminished responsibility. We said people who get married should sue each other for being so stupid . . . and then we realised, they do! Remember?'

'Just read one of the poems we did at school,' she replied. 'Oh yes, what about Slessor's "Five Visions of Captain Cook"?' I despaired. What had happened to Lola and how dare she rope me in on it? How is it possible that a previously black-wearing female atheist can reach her wedding day and suddenly feel the need to be blessed by God, before relatives she hates, while looking like a lolly snared in a mozzie net?

I rang Mrs James Swinton, nee Nicky Tilto, a distant friend and an honorary wedding specialist since she managed to convince her bridesmaids to wear orange bustles, and not one of them lost their life on the day. She suggested I read from a very popular non-religious 'alternative' wedding piece, which was written by Charles Sobhraj, Khalil Gibran or Karma Sutra, she couldn't remember quite whom.

I procrastinated for the month preceding the wedding, hoping to be debilitated in a freak yet painless accident. Unfortunately I wasn't kidnapped, and resolved to compose something myself about the beauty of the marital state; being a fiction writer I thought this shouldn't be too hard. I decided to speak about the notion of love, but discovered the word had lost a little of its gloss since it became the name of a brand of dog food. I looked up 'love' in a book of quotes and it said 'also see hate'; I looked up 'marriage' and it said 'also see divorce'. I looked up 'parenting' and it said 'also see poverty'. (This book was frighteningly accurate.)

In the end, I found the perfect piece, non-denominational, universal, whimsical, went down a treat (excerpt follows):

Thinking of you must be easy because I think of you all
the time,
Caring for you is easy because I think I care for you,
Having sex with you is easy because you really turn me on,

But promising that I will be with you forever is the easiest
    thing in the world,
Because I am in love with you and have gone completely
    mad.

(Hey, I should add a few 'ooh ooh baby's' and turn this
poem into an internationally best-selling pop song.)

motherhood is like passing
a camel through the eye
of a needle – and then having
to look after it for the
rest of your life

how to write a book

Many people aspire to write a book; the following is how a Writer actually does it. First, The Writer wakes one morning with a drought-breaking yearning once again to be creative. This usually manifests itself on a Saturday and reaches fruition, to public acclaim, in the kitchen that evening.

Assuming the meal is a culinary success, The Writer may wake again the following morning with a similar creative yearning. Depending on whether The Writer lives closer to an art shop or hardware store, Sunday's creative urge will produce out-of-whack bookshelves for the study or a post-modernist shemozzle, preferably in oils, on a too-large canvas in the living room. By Sunday evening the creative urge will have been replaced by artistic disillusionment. Early Monday morning The Writer will experience profound depression due to the realisation that his/her creative urge would have been better spent actually doing some writing. This will *creatively immobilise* The Writer (not to be confused with writer's block).

On Monday afternoon The Writer, no longer feeling at all creative, will decide a deadline is needed to inspire creativity and will ring his/her Publisher to announce the imminent arrival of his/her new book. Having thus confirmed the book's existence and scammed lunch for later that week, The Writer will feel creatively fulfilled and celebrate that night by drinking too much.

The following morning, with neither book nor idea, The Writer will wish that he/she was an accountant. This 'slump' will become the catalyst for the buying of useless knicky-knacky things for the rim of the bathtub, and this aesthetic indulgence will rekindle the creative urge, which The Writer will fulfil by proudly purchasing a note pad, a Biro, an HB pencil and one of those nice white erasers with the hard blue bit on the end. That night The Writer will not write because he/she is completely satisfied by the thought that at 6 a.m. the following morning he/she will at least commence, if not complete, the greatest novel known to humankind. At 6 a.m. the following morning the alarm will go off and The Writer will press the snooze button. Some time later The Writer will rise, shower, breakfast routinely, and sip self-loathing as he/she laments not rising at 6 because now the muse may be mute.

With two days to go before lunch with The Publisher, and no history of spontaneous combustion in the family, The Writer will be forced to seek creative inspiration. The note pad etc. will be taken to a cafe for the jotting down of whimsical life observations. During this time the book's dedication will be written and a thank you speech for the Booker prize.

On leaving, The Writer will bump into an old school chum, who will casually ask if 'you're still doing your writing', and it'll sound like the chum's being rude. Now The Writer will decide that what a writer needs is a lonely shack on a beach and . . . because The Writer doesn't have a lonely shack, The Writer obviously can't write. Feeling relieved that the book is finished before it's started, The Writer will take the dog for a walk and, while wearing a plastic bag as a glove, be struck by an Idea.

The Writer will then ring his/her Agent, divulge the idea and hear 'Mmm, sounds fab, but could you make it a bit more like *The Alchemist* meets *The Thornbirds*?' The Writer will then resolve never to share another creative thought with anyone and will ring a friend to talk about the Agent. This friend will respond so enthusiastically that The Writer will feel creatively fulfilled and have no need to write a book. So with one day before The Lunch, and nothing written, The Writer will postpone, saying he/she's 'on a roll' and the book's nearly finished.

At last, now with pressure postponed, The Writer is free to start writing. Driven by pride, the dollar and several acquaintances' much-lauded yet undeserving receipt of literary awards, each day thereafter is pretty well routine. Get up early, exercise, eat, switch on the computer, prepare to write, feel an overwhelming desire to lie on the floor and see if your feet can reach back behind your head. Ten minutes of writing, a cup of coffee, twenty minutes of writing, jog around the room, half a page completed and you simply must call . . .

The Writer will hate every moment of writing until, like hitting one's head against a brick wall, it feels so good when he/she stops. Text completed, the computer will collapse and the 'same-day technician' will return it in three weeks. Finally, The Writer will delightedly call his/her publishing house only to discover that it's been consumed by another publishing house, whose speciality is science-based coffee table books.

During the following three years The Writer will once again miraculously wake one morning with a drought-breaking yearning to be creative . . .

ageing gracelessly

You can rest assured that as soon as you begin to think your age sounds young, you're on the cusp of turning an age that sounds really old. It's my birthday and I'm having dinner with two theology students in a Californian-influenced Japanese restaurant in the Rocky Mountains of Colorado. Before we've even ordered our entrees the conversation has tumbled from the fat content of a pretzel to the real meaning of existence. At this point Hank retells the tale of Moses' forty-year walk through the desert, and I suggest that if he were a woman Moses would have saved a lot of time and just asked someone for directions.

Hank, who came to religion after a two-week Amway cruise, and is currently trying to grope my leg underneath the restaurant table, asks me how I feel about death and tells me that he's looking forward to his. I congratulate him, and tell him I'm looking forward to his death too, but am not yet ready for mine.

Meanwhile, twenty-year-old Nancy bubbles with a question. (During her 'I-am-a-Navaho-Indian' stage she changed her name to Running Water, but should have changed it to Drip.) Nancy came to religion because she's in love with Hank, and is currently either trying to grope him under the table or is urgently searching for a dropped dinner roll.

She asks me abruptly why I don't want to meet my Maker. And all I can think of is that I'm not old enough and I haven't got a thing to wear.

I want to ask, do I look that old, and then blame it on the lighting. And I want to say I haven't lived long enough; I'm not even ready to be an adult. I look at fifteen year olds and think that I'm them; I still blame my Mum for all my flaws. I haven't even mastered the simple things in life like flossing after every meal.

But when I was twenty, I thought even twenty-five was ancient, like Methuselah. I dated a bloke who was thirty-six, and every time we did anything vaguely physical I'd become scared he was going to drop dead.

At twenty-six, I had my tarot cards read and selected the Card of Ageing. 'Oh that's good,' said the reader, 'Ageing means wisdom.' And I thought 'Ageing, good? You must be joking, like having big childbearing hips!'

Then I turned thirty and I couldn't believe how one night's sleep could make me so much older. One day and I was a different generation, no longer young, no longer full of promise, no longer mucking around. I remember glancing in a shop window to see everyone around me was reflected but I was nowhere to be seen.

But the funny thing is now that I am older, I feel younger every day. Maybe there's been some mistake and I should check the birth certificate for typos. Maybe I really am twenty like Nancy, but then again why would I want to be? At twenty, I was an emotional wreck, unfocused, unhappy and unsure, with that dreadful song 'I've Been to Paradise But I've Never Been to Me' rattling through my head.

Youth is worshipped despite the fact that anyone beyond it knows it wasn't that good. Youth is worshipped for all it could be, not for all that it is. Life gets better, calmer, funnier – why then are the lines around my eyes not an envied status symbol?

I asked Hank how he felt about getting older and he said that, as a man, he felt great, but it must be horrible for me because I've reached 'that lonely side of the mountain that never gets the sun'.

Nancy agreed but added she hates being young because of all the unwanted attention. In fact, she's planning to chop off her long blonde hair because she's tired of the constant sexual approaches. (In response I asked politely if and when she chops it off, could I buy it from her?)

I go back to my hotel room where I'm swamped with best wishes because I've told absolutely everyone it's my birthday. (Last year I decided not to tell anyone and then got depressed when no one remembered.) As a birthday present the bellboy, who I'm sure is Dustin Hoffman, has managed to upgrade my accommodation to a room that has ventilation (not opening windows, because then I might jump and get away without paying my bill).

I've certainly had worse birthdays. When I was a kid my sisters revealed that they were organising a surprise party for me . . . and the surprise was that they weren't.

I ring the children, they sing me 'Happy Birthday' with a farting sound at the end of each phrase, and then I go to the bar for a quiet birthday drink. The doorman asks me for my ID, then says, 'Only joking.' I think only a woman of my age and maturity could possibly find that funny.

peas save me

Have you ever looked at a packet of frozen peas and read on the back 'For further information regarding this product we invite you to contact our website', and then have you wondered, who would contact a website about a frozen pea?

And then have you thought, am I missing something here? Maybe everyone wants to know about frozen peas and I've only just discovered echinacea? It's possible. Heaven knows what I was doing in the 1980s when the whole world loved colonic irrigation. (Oh, that's right, I was into Wham!)

Life is unpredictable; weird things happen. Just when you think you'll have a glass of chardonnay, you find it's passé and riesling is back in, because with the rate of change that exists today it is possible to live physically in 1998 with your mind embedded in a parallel universe that's on a several-year time-delay. So, as society runs towards a new millennium, the global *sujet de moment* could very well be the simple, little, green pea. (Honestly, if Melanie Griffith can get a Golden Globe nomination then the pea can also have its moment in the sun.)

My pea thing started a week ago, early in the morning. Zeke and Eppie were fighting as usual, or 'bonding' as I prefer to call it. 'Mum,' Eppie yelled, 'Zeke just called me an ugly, selfish witch!' 'Zeke, is that true?' 'Yes, Mum, it is, but I meant it in a really nice way.'

We were running remarkably on time, with at least two or three minutes up our sleeves to lose the car keys, remember forgotten homework, and mess up the tidied house. And that's when Ruby rang.

Ruby hasn't rung since her latest dysfunctional relationship started because Ruby's the sort of woman who dumps her female friends as soon as a bloke comes along. My immediate thought therefore was that her relationship must be over. 'No,' said Ruby, laughing hysterically in that cocky way people do who have just discovered good sex. 'No, we're having a dinner party and wondered if you might come.' (No thanks, I could think of nothing worse than being forced to watch two lovebirds perform culinary foreplay.) 'But there's someone we want you to meet.' (Why do coupled people try to couple up their single friends? Are they scared that otherwise we might tempt them back to our side?) No thanks, I can think of nothing worse than being X-rayed by some podunk who has bigger breasts than me. 'But this guy's gorgeous; you're made for each other.' And I don't know what happened, but we set a date. Gorgeous? This'll be good.

My usual babysitter wasn't available because she's in jail for theft and armed robbery, so a friend of hers volunteered to help. She arrived looking well aerated, with every protuberance pierced, and I realised I didn't trust this woman to shut the fridge and I was leaving her with my children. They liked her immediately, which is always a bad sign, and

I was considering ringing a babysitter to mind the baby-sitter when the blind date arrived to pick me up.

He arrived with a beanie over his head, and when I opened the door said, 'Stick 'em up.' I, of course, was meant to laugh, but I hit him with my shoe instead, and then when he removed the beanie to reveal a face that looked like my ex-husband's, I raised my shoe and hit him again and told him to take the garbage out. On returning he said good evening in such a silly voice that I spent five minutes talking the same silly way until I realised that he wasn't bunging it on. And that's when Ruby called to cancel and I told her I was suing.

'So you still want to have dinner?' he asked. Well, the babysitter's here for a minimum of four hours, because otherwise it's 'not worth her time' (like Linda Evangelista she obviously doesn't get out of bed for less than $10,000). So yes, I'll eat, I said, noticing his boating shoes and wondering when did boating shoes become acceptable casual attire, and why don't we dine out in ski boots? At the restaurant he talked about veganism, Buddhism and his rich family, and I imagined marrying him, killing him and spending his inheritance.

Then he told me he was on Prozac, and I asked if he had any and how long it took to kick in? And then he ate his food, and then he ate mine, and then we didn't speak for forty-five minutes until he said, 'Isn't it great that we can sit comfortably together without even saying a word.' And I thought this has possibly been the most boring night of my life and this guy's about to ask me to marry him! Made for each other? I think not, and so I paid the bill.

And then I walked home, paid the babysitter, and prepared to make myself dinner, but she'd eaten us bare and all I could find was a packet of frozen peas, which I read, then ate, then contacted on the Internet.

laugh?

A friend rings and says, 'Where do you find a tortoise with no legs? Where you left it.'

I don't laugh.

'What happened to your sense of humour?' she asks.

'I lost it,' I reply.

If the truth be told, I don't know if I lost it, if it was stolen, or if it just ran away, but nevertheless I reported it missing at two o'clock on Wednesday afternoon.

'I'd like to report a missing sense of humour.'

'Are you joking?' asks the police officer.

'I doubt it,' I reply.

'Well, can you perhaps describe it for us, Madam?'

'Yes, it's black and slightly bent.'

'Have you checked all the hospitals in your area?'

'It's not sick,' I say, slightly miffed.

'So when did you last see this alleged sense of humour?'

'Well, I had it last Saturday when I said something hilarious.'

'Do you have any witnesses who can verify its presence?'

'No, the friend I was with didn't think what I said was funny.'

'Well, what did you say?'

'I said, "What's a man's idea of foreplay? Half an hour of begging".'

'Your friend's right, that's not funny. Can you think of any other incidents where your humour may have been present?'

'Well, the night before my ex-husband called and I said, "You know it really wouldn't be bad if you contributed one cent to the rearing of the children." And apparently that was pretty humorous.'

'I see,' replied the officer. 'Do you have any reason to believe that your humour may perhaps have run away? Were you treating it unkindly, or abusing it at all?'

'No, but I did spend a weekend at a New Feminist seminar, so perhaps it was feeling neglected.'

'Is it possible that you may have simply misplaced your sense of humour, Madam?'

'Well, I've searched wherever I could have lost it, in all my old relationships, the queue at the bank, dinnertime with the kids, and on hold with directory assistance.'

'Any luck?'

'No. But I did find an old broken heart underneath the couch.'

'Could someone perhaps have borrowed your sense of humour?'

'Well, I did lend it to a friend for his office talent quest, but he gave it back to me the very next day, albeit somewhat warped.'

'Do you have any reason to suspect anyone might have stolen your sense of humour?'

'Well, there was a bloke the other night who seemed to find it attractive.'

'Was he behaving suspiciously in any way at all?'

'No. Except he made me pay half the bill, and when we left he said, "I'll call you", and then just started laughing.'

'Well, we haven't had any senses of humour brought in this week. A lot came in when John Howard came to power, but most of those had simply been abandoned.'

'So, what do you suggest I do?' I asked.

'You could check in the alleys, some are sold off the back of trucks but they're usually pretty filthy. Or failing that you could pick one up here, perhaps try an old one on for size.'

'Well, I don't want anything racist, sexist or otherwise bigoted.'

'Are you sure it's a sense of humour you want? We have a lot of discarded consciences here. They also tend to come in with a change of government.'

'No, I definitely want a sense of humour.'

'Well, the only ones we've got here all belonged to men.'

'Haven't you got just one female sense of humour?'

'Heavens no, they all get sold on the black market to Switzerland, Austria and Germany.'

'But I can't have a male sense of humour. I don't want to spend my life mocking people's speech impediments, laughing at penis and bum jokes, and hearing sexual double entendres even in a simple weather report.'

'I don't know, life's a lot easier if you can laugh at farts and breasts.'

I try on a male sense of humour.

'Here, let's see if it fits,' said the policeman. 'Why did

the housewife stare at the orange juice container from morning until lunch? Because it said Concentrate.'

I laughed. It fitted. I said, 'I see your point.'

'Oh, point! That would be a phallic reference. Get it, ha ha! Yes, that's really very funny.'

a friend in deed

Matthew calls. We've been friends for twenty years, but I told him that he'd put on weight, and now he's ringing to say he's not speaking to me.

I don't respond out of respect for Matthew because presumably if he doesn't want to speak to me he doesn't want to listen to me either. So he hangs up and rings back straight away to ask if I heard him the first time. I nod, which of course he doesn't hear, so two minutes later his secretary calls to confirm the fact that Matthew is not speaking to me. I decide that I shouldn't speak to his secretary either as she is sort of 'Matthew' in this communication, and so I nod to her on the phone as well. This drives Matthew insane so he faxes me an invoice for wasting his time. I don't respond, of course, because that would mean I'd have to charge him for my time, so he e-mails me to confirm I got the fax. I pass the fax on to my agent, who signs it on my behalf, returns it to Matthew but invoices him for 25 per cent commission. Matthew faxes my agent and tells them he will not pay and if they pursue he will sue. So we fax back that we'll counter-sue, which is problematic since other than being my friend, Matthew is also my lawyer.

It is at this point that Rebekkhah rings (she's one of those mutual acquaintances whom neither Matthew nor I are willing to claim). Rebekkhah's determined to reunite us because she's planning a dinner party to seduce some muscle-filled piece of lycra from her gym and wants us to fill the conversational void that will inevitably occur between the uttering of 'Hi Brad' and 'Gee, my back needs a rub'.

'What we need,' she says, 'is an Intervention to redeem your friendship.' Why we need to save a friendship that revolves entirely around my buying beers for Matthew (he's 'asset-rich but cash-poor') and listening to tales of his sexual conquests, which may I say were always pathetic and are still pathetic and would put even the antics of an hermaphroditic worm to shame, I do not know. But Matthew agrees because he thinks he might score with Rebekkhah and I agree because I need money and an Intervention sounds like something a government board might liberally offer grants or subsidies for.

Wrong. Apparently an Intervention is the latest thing from America and involves friends and relatives of the victim (drugs, alcohol, poor fashion sense) gathering and confronting him/her with his/her weakness and hugging them back to well-being. Not only is there no government assistance, but it is generally BYO (Jatz, cordial, elastic waisted culottes . . . whatever).

Matthew and I could have visited a relationship coun-sellor but unless I became his business partner, he couldn't make the visits tax deductible. So, Jenny (my friend), Duncan (his friend) and Iphigenia and Phil (our friends) organised to meet. (Rebekkhah couldn't come because she was at the gym.)

We meet at Jenny's house. I'm the first to arrive. Jenny's

crying because Brent, her live-in love of eight months, has suddenly removed himself from the house and taken the couch as well. Unlike Brent the couch was interesting, but I assure Jenny there'll be plenty more couches, and Duncan arrives next. Despite being an accountant by trade, he seems to be in a genuine state of excitement. Turns out he thinks he may be having an affair with a married woman. 'What do you mean "may be", you stupid bloody git!' says Jenny. 'How could you possibly not know?'

'Well, I mean, we got pissed and kissed on the stairs at Richard Tempston's party.' 'And?' demanded Jenny. 'And nothing,' replied Duncan. 'What? That's not an affair! That's not even a grope! That's just being dental floss.' 'But she said I was gorgeous.' 'Do you know her name or her number?' 'No, but I popped a love letter in her bag. And she sent it back today with the grammar corrected.'

Duncan opens the door to spot Phil and Iphigenia smiling in that way that perfect couples do when they're hiding 'a domestic'. Seems that Phil had found Iphigenia's old love letters. He's outraged at their passionate content and she's outraged at his invasion of privacy. 'Why did you keep them all?' he asks. 'I only kept the poetic ones,' she says, 'The others I sent back with corrections.'

Duncan collapses and the rest of us stuff ourselves with stress-consoling food. Stuff, stuff, stuff. Three hours later Matthew bounces in as skinny as he was in 1978, the stress of our dismembering friendship has obviously done him good. 'Sorry I'm late,' he says looking round the room. 'Boy haven't you all put on weight.' We don't answer because we're not speaking to him.

barking mad

Just reading about the new feminist: smart, savvy, sexy, likes her lipstick, knows her politics, speaks her mind, obviously destined never to get a bloke, when Elizabeth rings. 'High,' she says in the English accent she picked up while having a drink at the Royal Sydney Golf Club back in 1982. 'Guess wot?'

Well now, let me think, the last time she rang and asked this question she'd changed her name by deed poll to Sheikh. (It was meant to be Chic but she spelt it wrong on the form.) And the time before that she was ringing for technology advice: 'Do you think I should get a digital or a monologue mobile?' (Well, a digital's probably more conducive to conversation.)

The question 'Guess wot' obviously doesn't refer to her relationship because even though her husband, Hank, is so dull rumour has it that he's actually a hologram of someone who's dead, their finances are so inextricably bound they have to stay together. (Theirs was a shotgun wedding of course; you know, reach your mid-thirties, not yet wed, marry someone before you turn thirty-six or may as well shoot yourself.)

'You've lost weight?' I say. 'Oh, do you really think so?' she replies. 'You've bought more Telstra shares.' 'No, not yet.' 'You've got a new Jeep Cherokee and found a dirt road you can drive it on?' 'No.' 'All the council-protected gums in front of your house have suddenly died and miraculously expanded your harbour view?' 'No.' 'Your unborn child has won a scholarship to Oxford?' 'Nearly.' 'You're pregnant?' 'No, next best thing?' 'Next best thing to being pregnant? You've just given birth without pain, without stretch marks and without nine months of feeling like an inflated washing up glove?' 'Yes.' 'What?' 'Yes, we've bought a puppy! Say hello.'

I pause for a long time and then whisper 'Hello' as though telling someone that I love them on the phone while in a lift crowded with old boyfriends. In response Pooch wees on the handpiece and Elizabeth squeals. 'Isn't that cute?'

'What happened?' I ask. 'Did you get tired of all your other toys, the Stairmaster, the mountain bike, and the cute Latino gardener?'

'How dare you?' Elizabeth replies indignantly. 'Puppy's not a toy, he's like a child to me.' (Oh I see, one of those 'my pets are my children' people – what next, Mum and Dad numberplates?) So, you didn't endure pregnancy, its discomforts and associated traumatising fears, you can go for an entire week without bathing this 'baby', it will not need childcare at $10,000 per annum, you don't have to teach it real values and the meaning of existence while trying to embody those morals yourself, to feed it you just open a can, and when it's driving you insane you can lock it outside? You think for your 'baby' you'll go grey, sleep an average of ten hours every two years and become so proficient at applying contact adhesive to new exercise books that you could represent Australia at an Olympics? Child substitute. I don't think so!

(My uncle spent years teaching his parrot to say 'Polly wants a cracker'. And after five years the first words it said were 'Shut up'.)

So Elizabeth buys a dog to be her baby, obviously because dogs wag their tails when they're excited, just like she used to do. I think it's stupid, but then again who am I to doubt? Elizabeth is one of those dumb/smart people who appears for all the world to have the intelligence of a single sock, but knows what she wants and goes out and gets it, e.g. married for money, not love. I hate her, of course, because her life is simple joy, and the next joyful occasion, she sweetly informs me, is the pooch's Naming Ceremony. 'Please come, you'll just love him,' she says enticingly. 'He's honestly amazing, 'cause he's just like Hank.' 'Oh,' I reply, 'So he's neutered then.'

Their speed boat is called *Sue Purb*, their house is called La Maison, their lawyer is called Vacuum Cleaner (from his habit of picking up bits of fluff), so what are they calling the dog? I decide to go to the Naming Ceremony, although politically opposed. I don't like pets because all they do is eat, sleep and have sex, and to tell you the truth I'm jealous.

So what did they call him after all my cynicism? Spot, Rover, Blackie? No, they called him Hank Junior, after his father, and following the ceremony Hank Jnr made a brilliant short speech, danced with all the old aunts, had a beer with the blokes, played footy with the boys and skipping with the girls, hugged his parents, served the savouries, played Handel on the trumpet, and was the perfect child. And blow me down if by the end of the day I couldn't see that he was his father's son, although slightly better looking.

work hard,

play hard, live by

shoe slogans

phree willee

Several weeks ago I shared a dinner with my three surviving friends, i.e. those still remaining after the great marriage epidemic of 1994 and the extraordinary baby plague of 1996–98. The purpose of the dinner was to determine a simple way for the four of us to make an enormous amount of money and bring some meaning to our paltry, pathetic lives.

In attendance were: Me (desperately seeking financial status in a world where having occasionally glossy hair is simply not enough); Dosdon (formerly Brett, graduate of the now-defunct Australian Film Makers and Coffee Connoisseurs College, currently awaiting development funding on his 1981 award-winning short about a simple member of the filmic audience urgently racing through Hollywood blockbusters looking for a plot), Mary (recently abandoned mother of three, thinking of either doing a part-time psychology degree, selling Herbalife, or marrying the man who delivers the groceries because 'he's so reliable'); and Kenneth (sex lord and millionaire domestic cleaner who's wanting extra income in anticipation of a possible forthcoming need for bail).

And so we discussed our wealth-making plans. Mary suggested a lamington drive, Dosdon suggested we elevate him to guru status and create a tax deductible cult, and Kenneth proposed blackmail, kidnap, or international arms dealing.

We ruminated over staging a car accident and the discomfort of wearing a neck brace for three or four years until our case got to court, but finally settled on a far more profitable plan, infinitely better suited to our individual talents: the making of our own, shall we say, wildlife documentary, with catering by Mary and a script by me, directed by Dosdon, and starring Kenneth in the nude, cavorting with other nudies.

'Isn't that porn?' asked Mary.

'No, it's not, because pornography is designed to excite sexual pleasure and there's no way that watching Kenneth having sex is going to do anything but act as a sort of contraceptive.'

All right, so it is pornography, but pornography is a big money-earner nowadays and ever growing in public acceptance. (This has been aided by that video release by Pamela Anderson and Tommy Lee, a couple whose only dialogue during their first attempt at marriage appears to have been 'Oh, MY GOD'. Their family home-video taught us all that it is cool to handycam yourself having sex whilst steering a speeding boat through a crowded waterway using your big toe, but that it is stupid not to get the distribution rights.)

Add to this the ready availability of broadcast-quality video cameras, and you've got an avalanche of porn producers (including the ex-deputy chief censor).

The only problem the four of us faced at this point was just who would star with Kenneth. Lizzy, his long-term

girlfriend of two weeks, responded with 'A sex video starring Kenneth? What is it, a comedy?' Shorna, his ex-wife,
replied similarly but replaced the word 'comedy' with
'tragedy'. And Tanya, a spokesperson on behalf of all his
former partners said, 'I don't think Kenneth should have a
co-star, because he can actually do the whole thing
himself.'

'Why don't we hire someone to act with Kenneth?'
Dosdon suggested. 'We could use the money we're saving
on costumes.'

'Well, if we hire someone,' piped in Mary, 'why can't it
be Kayak?' (Think kayak, canoe, Keanu.)

'Hey,' I responded. 'If it's Keanu, I want to be in it too.'

'Why do you both want to romp nude with Keanu and
never want to romp nude with me?' asked Dosdon, scratch-
ing his croissant moustache.

'Umm, well, Dosdon, why don't we hire someone for
you?'

'You mean like a porn queen?'

'No, I mean a body double.'

Kenneth and Dosdon questioned the joy of such vicari-
ous involvement, but were satisfied when asked to write
our little film's script. 'More women,' they were heard to
scream excitedly as they typed.

We changed our names to make them pornographically
correct, and then Rock Hard, Tad Bigger, Cheek E. Butt and
I (Bust Woman) watched our film collapse. We couldn't
afford even the smallest piece of Keanu, my liposuction was
put on a waiting list for elective surgery (instead of the
emergency it so obviously was), and Mary got back with

her pathetic husband, who insisted they play the married couple in our film. What, eating burnt chops, watching teev?

So we don't have a film but what we do have is the title, *Phree Willee* (which avoids copyright through the art of misspelling), and we're willing to sell it for a fortune.

it's a man's world

I was feeling rejected, so I rang a therapist, but he never returned my call. So then I resolved to be 'really nice to people'. It lasted two days until I got bored. Finally I decided to start this week's piece with 'the following column will be rather short as I've decided to become a painter', but the phone rang right then and there, so I once again had something to write about.

It was Bachelor Ben.

'Guess what? I'm getting married!'

'Oh that's fantastic. Who to?'

'I don't know,' he said.

Now I've known Ben since we were kids and lived next door to each other. He was the first boy I kissed, the first boy I shared a bath with (and sadly he was also the last), and we always said that we'd marry each other when we both grew up. But life intervened, I ran off to Italy to be a 3D cliché, chasing cute foreign boys who didn't speak English in the belief that not understanding a word someone says actually makes them more interesting. And Ben, of course, became a sports commentator on commercial TV and consequently never grew up at all.

Over the years he has dated the equivalent of a small island population, all husky-voiced and, at least ultimately, blonde. One of them was actually really quite clever, but she was so smart she left him.

Ben got pissed a lot, made a squillion and became 'a legend'. He drove fast cars, shook hands with PMs and smooched openly with post-pubescent soapie stars, but in that time he never married and appeared to be allergic to the concept. He dated, he dumped. He fell in love at first sight with one beautiful girl but when she burped loudly after skolling a beer, he got a strange inkling that she was a fella and so he had to dump him as well.

Such an incident could have put him off intimate female relations altogether, but to his credit he kept on trying, again and again and again. And now he's thirty-nine and says he wants to get married. 'How come?' I ask with all the charm of someone accusing the butcher of selling bad ham. 'Nothing sinister,' he replied. 'It's just my biological clock.'

Oh yes, men have biological clocks as well, but unlike a woman's, which is wound by an instinctive desire to nurture, a man's is triggered, as he approaches his forties, by the looming prospect of spending old age alone, and his instinctive need to be nurtured.

'Why don't you just go to a nursing agency?'

'Are the girls there good-looking?'

Of course, every female knows this need to be nurtured is chromosomally apparent in males; it raises its head when he has a cold, or the TV reception fails during the footy, but during the earlier years of life a male human's needs can be fully satisfied with a simple bowl of chips or a smile from a stranger (assuming she has large breasts).

Indeed it is only as a male's hair begins to thin and his

sex drive starts to wane that a man may require more permanent nurturing, of the marrying kind. 'Quick, to the trenches,' cries the testosterone as the blokes stand in the human battlefield of life and realise they are growing defenceless. Once you've got your real estate and your shares, you need a wife as an investment.

If I were a bloke I'd do the same. Indeed as a woman I do! I plan to settle down at about eighty-three, and even that notion is disposable if Matt Damon is still out there dating.

'Ben, do you mind me asking what sort of woman you think you're going to marry?'

'I want a career girl, someone well-educated, smart, attractive and independent, with a life of her own.'

'Well, if she has all of those things, why would she want you? To sire her children, perhaps? And after that she'll divorce you, and then you'll be poorer than ever, and an even less attractive catch. What you really need is someone stupid or desperate. Perhaps you could ask if your mates have any sisters.'

'My mates wouldn't let me marry any of their sisters!'

We placed an ad in the paper, in both the personals and classifieds. Ben wrote a brief description of himself and it was complete and utter rot – describing himself as supportive and attractive, he sounded like a Wonderbra. We got a few calls from the Philippines and one from an all-male jail in Texas.

But it's about time Bachelor Ben grew up and understood that long-term love is hard to find, and you don't just click your fingers when you've had enough of singledom and have the perfect member of the opposite sex ready and just waiting to adore you.

The phone rings. I hope it's the therapist – but it's Claudia Schiffer wanting Ben.

PMT (dynamite!)

My Levis will no longer do up, which would suggest I've put on weight but, bugger it, I'm blaming the jeans. Yep, either the jeans have done something they definitely shouldn't have, or else they've been stolen and quietly replaced by some inferior others – in the same way Dezlee's personality's been swapped with some absolutely appalling mess that also doesn't fit.

She's at the door, looking like a cross between Bernard King and a retired regional lawn bowls champion, wearing tracksuit pants and a red sequinned bolero. She clutches a Mars Bar, Cadbury Family Block, two packs of Tim Tams and an empty jumbo-size hot chip bucket. Her face is purple and rather puffy – apparently she couldn't remember where she parked her car this morning so she ran the 9 kilometres to my house. Something's not right. Dezlee's not a fit chick. The nearest she's ever gone to a 'sit-up' is a 'getting-up' off the couch to get a ciggy. Oh I get it, Dezlee's got PMT! Well, who let her out on her own?

'You haven't been shopping today?' I ask gently. 'And if you have, did you keep the receipt?'

'Yes, I have been shopping, I threw out the receipts and I'm wearing my new outfit now.'

'Oh my God,' I mumble softly.

'What?' she says. 'Do you think I look fat?'

I panic. 'You haven't rung anyone today, have you?'

'No. Why, what's the matter?'

'Oh I'm just relieved you haven't phoned your boss this morning to tell him how stuffed your job is.'

'Heavens no, I told him that yesterday.'

Dezlee's laughing as she enters the house. I ask how she is and she says fine, then collapses in tears. The last time this happened she was giving a speech at the Business Woman of The Year lunch. She was asked to speak about her success and spent forty minutes on the podium asking the audience for advice on her hair.

The kids ask if we can hose her (too many years of living with a labrador who was sexually obsessed with the couch) but now Dezlee's stopped crying and wants to talk about life, love and loneliness. It'd be perfect if this were *Oprah*, but it's the middle of my daughter's seventh birthday party.

This birthday has been an issue from the start. My daughter wanted a rock 'n' roll party. I said the house is too small for rock 'n' roll, how about all your friends come over and stand really still and we'll have a rock party instead.

She wanted something pretty. I said her friends could come as brides. She said she wanted to have her party outside. I said we'll have it at the beach. She said you can't have a bride party on the beach. And my Mum said, 'I've got the solution, why don't all your friends come dressed as something that you might find on the beach (what, like a fabulously chiselled, Adonis-like muscle-man) . . . like an old beer bottle or a fish head.'

And now ten little girls, all dressed as fairies, are sitting on my kitchen floor watching this red-nosed, unkempt harridan unfurling the sort of frightening tirade that one normally sees on World Wrestling.

'I want you all,' Dezlee says to the seven-year-olds, 'to leave your jobs, leave your schools and, if need be, leave your families, because I have an important goal for you this year, and that is to find me a man.

'But then again,' she continued, 'what's the point? You meet them, you have great sex, you fall in love, you hang out together, you have less sex, you run out of conversation, the relationship's over, but you can't leave 'cause you've invested too much time, so you get married, are briefly thrilled, then you're sad again, but you can't leave 'cause you now share a mortgage so you have three kids instead and stay miserable together for the rest of your lives for the sake of the children.

'A woman's life,' she concluded, 'is a disaster. We want a career, we want our freedom and yet we want children and marriage. No man can equal the superwomen we are; we're doomed to a miserable lonely existence: overworked, over-looked and over it!'

I was appalled. Since conception I've taught my daughter to be strong, brave and smart. At the age of five she received her first Barbie, and we dressed her up as Xena instead.

What had Dezlee done to these girls? Depressed them, distressed them, made them aspire to be the women who point to prizes in game shows.

I looked at their faces; they all grinned from ear to ear.

Some little fairies began to clap and some began to cheer, and my daughter leaned close to whisper keenly, 'Can we get this clown back next year?'

dick dangler

An opportunity arose to abseil down one of Sydney's taller buildings. The building in question was thirty-six floors high, but for the benefit of the story we'll say it was 243.

Now, I've never abseiled before in my life. I descended from a balcony at a cocktail party recently but apparently the technical term for that is 'plummeting'. I don't even know people who abseil, well not anyone who's still alive. (Some people I know regularly rock-climb but, rather than being an act of bravery, I think we all realise that, with official holds called 'jugs' and 'nobs', rock-climbing's just a primitive sex substitute.) I'm scared of heights, I don't look good in a harness, and the last thing I need is a substitute for sex (when I've got all this ironing to do). So what did I say when invited to abseil? I said, full of breathy, panting excitement, 'Yes . . . yes . . . yes!'

Why? Well, first, because it was a charity fundraiser, second, because I wanted to conquer my fear, and third, because I was thoroughly assured that I wouldn't have to do a thing except entrust my life to some bloke and a rope! And that was the carrot, the simple fact that for a few minutes of my life I would not only not be responsible for anyone else, but that someone else would be responsible for me!

I, like many, lead my life being relentlessly in charge of

others, answerable for their punctuality, their cleanliness, their obnoxious behaviour – and that's just accounting for my friends. So accustomed am I to being responsible that if the guy collecting the bridge toll looks unhappy I perceive it to be my fault.

Abseiling; how carefree, and I didn't have to prepare a thing – no costume to construct or lamingtons to make, just simple me in something other than a skirt, and shoes with very good grip (I did do some preparatory sit-ups, but they made me look fatter so I stopped).

Now, despite being in that age group that I like to refer to simply as 'post-trainer bra', on the day of the descent I was full not of fear but rather 'giggly excitement'. This was aided by the thinning air and also my fantasies regarding my co-climber (or professional escort as they're called, unless my mother is in earshot). I imagined he'd be a tall, wise, young but mature, loving, educated, artistic, trav-elled, humorous, handyman/*cordon bleu* chef whose back I'd somehow be straddling, like a baby koala, as we abseiled down to heaven.

I thought we'd court each other on the descent and then spend the rest of our lives together – that is until I actually met him. It wasn't his T-shirt that offended me, although it read 'Just because I slept with you last night, it doesn't mean I have to abseil with you today'. No, what repelled me was his voice. (I was so distressed I wanted to cancel, but was inspired to continue by the bloke who fitted my harness and told me it made me look slim.)

We set off. Revolting One's job was to 'talk me down', but I tried to ignore his voice. Think of something else, I said to myself, get panic-struck by the prospect of a violent wind hurtling you through a plate-glass office-window and into a large fish tank where you remain, wearing nothing but your shredded clothes and exposed old maternity underwear, until you're finally discovered after a long weekend and are arrested for indecent exposure.

But I couldn't help myself. That voice made me sick and I realised why when it said, 'Come on chicken legs, move your arse!' The voice belonged to Noël Schmill, my nemesis from primary school. Now was my chance to seek revenge – for the severed plaits, the cruel nickname 'Vomit', the Dragstar bike-wheel imprint that still scars my leg. I could kill him! I could say it was an accident (but then he wouldn't really suffer). I could kill myself, and make it look like his fault, then he'd suffer for the rest of his life! (but then I wouldn't be around to see it).

The moment I'd dreamt of had finally arrived, but we were down to the seventy-eighth floor and time was running out. He was beside me, hanging from his rope. I resolved to swing behind him, clasp his neck with my knees, reveal my identity, then taunt and tease him until he begged for his life and apologised profusely for all that he'd done when we were nine. But then I remembered those famous words: 'A man that studieth revenge keeps his own wounds green', and I decided to behave responsibly. Damn it!

So I did nothing, but as I landed I fell and grossly bloodied my knee. Noël laughed at me convulsively, then when he stopped I said, 'Hey that was really great, let's go down together again.'

the mother of all days

A four-wheel drive company is now making sunglasses. I wonder if they're also for people who don't need them. Maybe I'll get some for Mother's Day.

Last Mother's Day I received a packet of musk incense, which I'm allergic to, and a broken musk-scented bath soap. *Mes enfants* didn't actually give them to me; I found them in that compost pit at the bottom of their schoolbags, two days after I'd given my children five dollars each to go and buy me a present! All up, my Mother's Day booty cost me $20. Let me explain.

At our local school every occasion is a possible moneymaker because we don't have overflowing coffers. (In fact, much to my horror, we don't even have pretentious school stickers to adhere to the back windscreens of our motor vehicles as the social-climbing equivalent of exposing oneself and having a public fiddle.) So anyway, every year Mother's Day is a fundraiser in the form of The Mother's Day Stall. Each child, i.e. mother, contributes a gift, and then each child, with the mother's money, buys a present to take home to Mother. The art, if you contribute something nice, is to make sure your child buys it back.

On the other hand, should you contribute something

tacky, i.e. dead Aunty Jean's congealed talcum powder, the art is in ensuring that the item is wrapped beyond recognition and that your child understands that if he/she brings the thing home again it will be placed in his/her Santa sack next Christmas.

The Mother's Day before last the car ran out of petrol and then blew up. It's quite easy, you see, to confuse your car's petrol gauge with your car's temperature gauge. So you think that your engine is running nice and cool and your petrol consumption is simply fantastic until you're left stranded with two children and your mother, 23 kilometres from anywhere because, as a special Mother's Day treat, you thought you'd take them for a relaxing drive in the country to get away from it all. (I remember we finally found civilisation in the form of a golf course. There we spotted a lone fellow furiously whacking the ball, then literally running to the next shot, only to furiously whack the ball again and set off at a sprint once more. I recall wondering what he did for a living and thinking, he's probably an obstetrician.)

Ah, Mother's Day, the celebration of the holiest of roles. One day a year dedicated to that goddess who gave her figure that you might live – the woman we abuse, over-work, manipulate and resent for all but the time between her serving the family lunch on that second Sunday in May and doing the washing up straight after. (My mother gives *me* a present on Mother's Day. Last year it was a folk-art painting of a coiled clay ashtray.)

Last week a pregnant friend asked for my advice on motherhood. Now I'm usually flattered by people who ask for my advice (unless I'm employing them as my accountant or lawyer), but on this occasion I was floored because most mornings I wake and the first thought that comes to mind is the simple word, 'Help'.

Mistakes? No, I've never made any – deviations we like to call them, for example a bedtime story I told the kids when exhausted one night, 'Once there was a magic man, but then he died. There now, go to sleep.'

But I do my best. On my daughter's birthday I enquired if there was anything she'd like to ask me, woman to, er, small woman. She was excited, thought for a while, and then solemnly said, 'Do you need a licence to wear stilettos?'

My son then asked if he could ask a question. About women? Oh my God! I was planning on getting all my knowledge at his school sex-education night when he's about eleven. 'Mu-u-um?' 'Yes?' I squeaked. 'Who do you think's the best half-back in the world?' 'Oh, that's easy,' I said with relief, 'that'd be one of the Chappell brothers, probably Ian, I think.'

I asked Mum for her motherhood advice, although I have been known to blame her mothering skills for my entire life – but she just said some Calvin Trillan line about the mother who served leftovers for thirty years, but the original meal was never found.

So, all alone, late at night, I wrote down everything I've learnt in the past ten years, and discovered there are only five things: learn the difference between your fuel and heat gauges, don't demand-feed, trim your daughter's hair regularly (to make it grow thicker), try to refer to fruit and vegetables as 'junk food' (because it's the only

way your kids will eat them), and, for Mother's Day, just
get your kids to wrap something that you already own —
it'll immediately save you a fortune and you know you'll
get something you want.

and now for the future

I had a dream. And I have seen the future. The future is sponsored by a Feminine Hygiene Product, presented to you by *Hey Hey It's Saturday* (format still unchanged), and hosted by a cloning merge of Natasha Stott Despoja and Rex Hunt. (The future's likeable, reliable, trustworthy role models will all be clones of those we have at present.) The future's most powerfully performing stock will be Ray Martin DNA Inc.

In the future, 90 per cent of our parliamentarians will be former Gold Logie winners, much of Australia will be up for lease as a 'rubbish tip' for international garbage disposal, more than half the population will know the words to 'Advance Australia Fair', and our national symbol will be the pokie machine.

In the future, the word 'absolutely' will be rationed, it will be illegal to take a great song from the past and use it as an advertising jingle, people who personally endorse a product will have to prove that they actually use it, and Michael Jackson's nose will fall off.

In the future, war will be deemed a sport and subsidised by the selling of broadcast rights. Multinational corporations will sponsor troops and fight to have naming rights. Helmets, flak jackets, exposed body parts and 'ammo' will all be viewed as potential advertising space.

In the future, instant coffee will become retro-cool, jet-skis will be laughingly remembered in the same breath as beta video recorders, and the value of the Australian dollar will be directly linked to the health, weight and current performance of the Australian cricket captain.

In the future, there will be a rush on tattoo removals, the European Union will collapse, and someone will probably invent that blue dye that's meant to follow you around when you wee in a public pool.

In the future, people who have only met you once will not have the right to say they 'know you'.

In the future, we will understand that anyone who tells you gossip will be gossiping about you next.

In the future, journalistic sources referred to as a 'close friend', 'former associate', or 'long-time acquaintance' will have to identify themselves.

And in the future, people will take plastic bags for a walk, and leave out the complicating dog element altogether.

In the future, strangers will tell you if you have parsley on your teeth, shoulder-pads will make a brief reappearance, urban vehicles with bull bars will be classed as lethal weapons, US sitcoms will be classified as Australian television content, and one-minute noodles will take thirty seconds.

In the future, no one will ever actually answer a telephone and our voice-mails will do deals in our absence, GPs will pay us for the time we're kept waiting, and adolescent heads will slowly evolve to face the same direction as their caps.

In the future, airline food will still taste exactly the same.

In the future, men will react to the achievements of feminism. For a brief period of time they'll discuss forming a men's movement to reassert their power but their plans for world domination will quickly collapse when the menfolk can't find a woman who'll organise it for them.

In the future, female netballers will earn more than rugby league players, washing machine repairmen will turn up on time, teaching and nursing will become the highest paid occupations. Courtney Love will become the US President, and there will be a world class-action against muzak on the grounds of mental cruelty.

In the future, life will be childproof.

In the future, Australia's wealthy will glean more kudos through visibly sponsoring public hospitals and schools than endlessly acquiring luxury cars and accumulating vacuous millions.

In the future, the fad of retirement will pass, age will be respected, and we will recognise youth for the mirage that it is.

Alternatively, in the future, super-models might rule the world.

In the future, newspaper 'corrections' will be located on the same page number as the original inaccurate information.

In the future, Australia's principal source of revenue will be parking fines, women will fight for the right to stay at home and raise their children, Crowded House will reform, then Crowded House will disband, then Crowded House will reform, then Crowded House will disband . . .

In the future, people will avoid human replacement technology, and humans will become fashionable.

In the future, 'Now' will be produced as a blockbuster musical.

school dysfunction

The following article was submitted under duress for publication in my school's Old Girl magazine, *Wittagi* (meaning 'battleaxes'). N.B.: Dates have been changed to protect my complexion.

Well, another camaraderie-filled reunion celebrated by the class of 1980 (and may I say how good it was actually to be invited this year). First, apologies from those unable to attend: from Lynette (voted Superwoman of the Year in 1991, 1992, 1993 and 1994, and now living in a mental asylum in Crickwell); from Dana (who was unable to attend for personal reasons, see accompanying newsletter for details); and, of course, from Elizabeth, whom we sadly understand has suffered a tragic liposuction accident (as fat as Demis Roussos in his heyday, they say).

On another note, congratulations must go to Mrs John Trotter (formerly known as Sue Can't-get-a-bloke Brown), who not only managed to get a bloke bearing remarkable similarities to a famous TV star (Homer Simpson), but who also organised the entire BYO gala event for a mere $75 a head, provided sumptuous curled-vegetable nibblies with dip, got her blond-ringleted children to serve the delicacies, and did so all in the glorious intimacy of her own

Tuscan-inspired, country-toned, Tudor-conversion home.

Congratulations also to Mrs John Trotter for her inaugural school reunion showbag. What a novelty and well worth the $7.50. The cassette of Sue singing our old school anthem was of course priceless, as was the Frozen Moment school lunch, and the fabulous wear-anywhere 'Wodenscroft Class of 1980' T-shirt. (May I say I have always wanted to wear my age emblazoned upon my back and chest and I am veritably thrilled to bits at the thought of now being able to spend the rest of my days hearing people say 'Gee, I thought you were older.')

Congratulations are also extended to those married women who attended the function and enquired after the romantic status of the single women present without saying, 'Oh my God, I'm sorry to hear that.'

Congratulations to Evelyn Crisp, Alison Knightly and Tara Bennett for marrying so well, to Jennifer Halworth for miraculously getting rid of her crow's feet, and to Fran Lidcombe for having the bravery to bring her 'friend' Deirdre along.

Thank yous must again go to Mrs John Trotter for the entertainment provided by her three adorable blond-ringleted children with their beautiful rendition of the entire *Sound of Music* soundtrack (an amazing achievement, particularly when they should have been in bed hours ago).

Finally, while on the formalities of the evening, requests for forgiveness have been received on behalf of the Trotters' golden labrador, Goldy, who, as we all know, tried to have sex with every object at the function (both animate and inanimate), and apologies are extended to Heather Miston's fur coat, with which Goldy actually succeeded.

All in all, the night was a huge success. Old friendships were vociferously rekindled, handshake deals were secured by the menfolk, home-help and stock tips were exchanged by the women, and the delightful omnipresence of the blond-ringleted Trotter offspring was a comforting reminder to the childless among the gathering that perhaps they hadn't made the wrong decision after all.

Personal highlights included moments with Cathy Ferguson and her husband of eight years, with whom I shared a very intimate conversation about the difficulties they're encountering choosing a new roller-door for their triple garage.

Also, if I may, I'd like to take this opportunity to conclude a few unfinished conversations. Caz, re: *The Women's Weakly, Hey Hey* Win-a-Holiday Competition, I'm not sure of the answer to 'What is the missing letter in chocol_te', but have you tried 'a'? Leanne, I believe the headmistress would be honoured if you named all your children after her; and Peter Maxell (husband of Mrs Peter Maxell, formerly known as Sarah Spittle), I think your film idea sounds interesting, however, perhaps the title, *Titanic 2*, needs some work.

Last, but not least, thanks to the neighbours for tolerating such a safari of Range Rovers parked upon their lawns, to the police department for being so understanding when the high-pitched squeals uttered by the female guests as a traditional greeting call repeatedly set off the local shopping mall burglar alarms, and of course thank you to the fabulous Katy

Leesham, who was caught in a, shall we say, compromising position with Mr John Trotter and who, as a result, has generously given us something to talk about at the next reunion. Until then.

pique hour

My cousin Michael rang at domestic peak hour. My daughter was in the middle of reciting the list of foodstuffs she couldn't possibly eat for dinner (vegetables, pasta, rice, cheese, meat, chicken, fish, bread or fruit), while my son, already having informed me that he is now a vegetarian and therefore can only eat sausages, was seated at the other end of the kitchen table diligently writing his homework list of 'Useful Creepy Crawlies' (leeches provide anti-coagulation and maggots help fertilise the soul [sic]).

Normally it's my mother's function to ring at domestic peak hour. 'Mum, I can't talk now, I'm really stressed.' 'Oh, do you want to talk about it?'

But this time, as I said, it was Michael. 'What's the matter?' I asked hurriedly. 'Do you need further instructions on how to use a can opener?'

'No, it's Evangeline.' Evangeline is the woman he met at the local Porn and Prawn Night. (She wasn't participating in the porn segment of the evening. She was serving fried chicken wings dressed as a prawn.)

'Michael, I really can't talk right now, can I call you back?' My hated call-waiting begins to beep. (Mum gave me call-waiting for my last birthday because she thinks it's disrespectful to have an engaged signal that forces callers to

persist until I deign to be free. How it can be more respectful to interrupt one call to see if another is more interesting
or important I do not know, but anyway.) 'I'll hold,'
Michael replies.

I answer the call to discover it's my kids ringing from
the kitchen on my mobile. 'Mu-u-um, when will dinner be
ready?' I hang up, which makes no difference because I can
still hear them yelling down the hall.

Son tells daughter she doesn't understand life, which he's
told her since she was two, and daughter tells son that he is a
racist because 'some people like to eat meat, you know!'

I return to Michael. Call-waiting beeps again. I excuse
myself and prepare to yell at the children but a fax comes
through instead. It's from Mum and says she's been trying
to get through on the telephone but our call-waiting's been
engaged. She's going to make enquiries tomorrow to see if
you can't get call-waiting-waiting.

Michael. The last time he sounded this traumatised was
when I pooh-poohed his theory of how to meet females at
parties. 'All you do,' he'd suggested, 'is stand outside the
women's toilet and meet them when they exit.'

'Michael,' I said, 'that's not going to help you get a date!
Women are desperate on their way *into* the toilet, not on
their way out.'

I began to feel tired. Did I really want to talk about
Evangeline? The kids needed their dinner, Mum was about
to get RSI through pressing the redial button, and what
had Michael ever done for me, except try to sell me in 1978
while on a family holiday in Budgewoi?

I excused myself to check on the children, who were

suddenly being excruciatingly quiet. I found my daughter staring at a whole onion, trying to make herself cry, and I found my son illustrating his homework while lying on my bed. 'Did you draw on my doona?' I yelled.

'No,' he replied. 'The Texta did.'

I returned to the phone, Michael was still there and a new call-waiting was beeping. I took the call. It was a wrong number. 'Okay, Michael, what's the problem?' Call-waiting beeps again. I take the call, scream and hang up.

'Well, last night I went to Evangeline's house. We were sitting by the fireplace admiring her new budgie when it flew onto my shoe and somehow I kicked it into the fire.'

I encouraged Michael to keep talking while I ran off to put the kid's dinner on the table, then I returned to the phone and a persistent call-waiting. It was Mum. I told her I was on the phone to Michael and would call her straight back, then I told Michael to give Evangeline a peace offering, perhaps some Pyrex plates because they're heat resistant. 'Can I go now?' I then asked. (The children had both finished their dinner but were refusing to have a bath because 'you can't go in the water when you've only just eaten'.)

'No,' says Michael. 'You can't go now, I've got someone here who wants to talk to you.' It's Mum; she's driven over to Michael's 'cause she couldn't get through to my phone. She wants to know what I'd like for Christmas — after all it's June already.

Call-waiting begins to beep. I answer. It's Telstra wanting to know if I'd like more phone services connected. I try to hang up, but do something wrong and Telstra ends up talking to my mother. Relief, now I don't have to deal with either of them, but I bet I know what I'm getting for Christmas.

ski bunnies

I have a pair of black tracksuit pants with fluoro-orange stripes down each side. They make me look like I'm moving really fast even when I'm sound asleep, snoring on the lounge. I also have a pair of sunglasses that make me look like I can ski, and I blame them for last weekend.

Actually, it started on the Wednesday. I was wearing my sunnies, caught my image in the reflective oiled biceps of a gym junkie in the queue at my local supermarket, and thought, 'Oh my God, look at me, I look like a professional skier. Why not take the seven-year-old down to the snow and teach her how to ski?'

Now, I ski like a potato. I have the technical know-how and I've chalked up the miles, but basically *après* skiing's my thing, outfitted to the eyeballs, sitting in a bar. (The last time I tried to put on a ski boot I actually sprained my ankle.)

So anyway, come the Friday, Eppie and I are dressed in our parkas and a heatwave kicks in. Eppie asks sweetly if we can go to the beach but I put my sunglasses on (like skiing legend Tomba La Bomba) and tell her 'No, we're going skiing.'

The drive is long, slow and stinking hot and all I can hear is that monotonous drone 'Are we there yet? Can I have something to eat?', and tragically the voice is my own. After four hours of this torture Eppie needs serious cheering-up so I stop and buy a junk-food display. She eats the lot, laughs and sings, and then vomits all over the car.

I clean the interior (my, what a blessing to have woollen car-seat covers at a time like this) and we continue our journey at a steady 110 kilometres per hour as I wonder how trucks speed limited at 100 kilometres per hour are overtaking us. I kick in the cruise control, which means my foot falls asleep, and I entertain myself by asking Eppie to recall what it was like in the womb. Very nice, she informs me enthusiastically, but there aren't really many good toys.

We stop for petrol and a lovely man gives us a cassette titled 'Safe Driving Tips'. The gift sends Eppie straight to sleep and I'm just nodding off when the cassette jams in the player and I career off the road trying to extricate it using the arm of my sunglasses.

An hour later we stop at Jindabyne to collect our hire skis. We put them on the roof and forget to fasten them. We find all the bits, return them, replace them, and drive on singing 'What the World Needs Now is Love Sweet Love' as I put my sunglasses back on.

It's getting dark; I take my sunglasses off. We arrive in Thredbo and it starts to rain. Next morning, it's still pouring, any snow is melting and there's not a soul in sight. I start to sulk until I recall Laurence J. Peter's inspiring words, 'There are two sorts of losers – the good loser, and the one who can't act', and I put my sunglasses back on.

Eppie insists she wants to learn to ski, and we discover she has two left boots. I fork out a fortune and hire more boots. Then Eppie sits on her goggles and breaks them in half so I fork out more money to replace them. Then I fasten her helmet and ski boots, secure her mittens, parka and braces, tuck in all six layers of clothing, and say, 'Okay baby, let's go skiing!' and she says 'I need to go to the toilet.'

Weary, we stop for lunch. Then the rain turns to hail as we venture up the mountain, and then the hail turns into a blizzard. (I remember Dave Barry's inspiring words, 'Skiing combines outdoor fun with knocking down trees with your face.') Once at the top Eppie and I spend an hour in the First Aid hut pretending we have stomach-aches so the attractive ski patrollers will let Eppie share the warmth of their room and let me fantasise about being rescued by all the cute blokes (without the cold, painful, scary bit that usually comes before the pleasure of their company).

I prepare psychologically for the downhill run by recall-ing a short story by Roald Dahl on the subject of pain, fear and death, and Eppie plays 'I spy with my little eye some-thing the colour of white'.

When the weather momentarily clears, I discover my skis have disappeared. (They're really long skis, in a wonderful silver colour, designed specially to look fab on top of the car.) I put on my sunglasses and at last see a guy who's confused his skis with mine. (He's wearing gear with the brand name Swankair. But I don't see the 's'.)

Finally, exhausted, Eppie and I catch the last lift of the

day all the way down the mountain. Snuggled together Eppie says, 'But Mum, I haven't learnt to ski!'

'Don't worry darling,' I whisper in her ear, 'I'll let you borrow my sunglasses.'

girls' knights

The phone rings, it's tragic Leonard again. Having tried
unsuccessfully to meet sweet and nurturing young women
(i.e. nurses) by feigning a sprained ankle and, having admit-
ted himself to Casualty, he's ringing to seek 'babe advice'.

'I'm sorry Leonard, I can't talk now. We're in the middle
of our weekly Girls' Night.'

'Oh perfect,' Leonard says. 'I'll be right over.'

Girls' Nights have long been the subject of male curios-
ity. Most men, driven by the thought that women can't
possibly have an enjoyable time without at least one phal-
lus present, presume that Girls' Nights revolve solely
around getting pissed and finding blokes to worship, e.g.
strippers who are so gorgeous they're obviously gay and
hence no threat to the heterosexual menfolk waiting at
home befriending microwaved tuna casserole while watching 'The Footy Show'. (Why did God invent men? Because
sex toys can't mow the lawn.)

But Leonard is one of a quaint male minority that does
not believe a Girls' Night requires men. No, he believes
Girls' Nights must only have women . . . preferably
disrobed and massaging each other with a mixture of oil
and mud . . . all the while softly cooing (insert relevant
male name here, e.g. Leonard).

Well normally, of course, we girls do romp naked whilst sipping lo-joule champagne but this week in a surprising break with tradition we'd assembled to discuss (a) our individual investment portfolios, (b) a proposed all-girls swim to the coast of Cuba (obviously Susie Maroney-inspired and so much cheaper than flying), (c) a legal class action by all the women of the world against Viagra, and (d) the pain incurred when one accidentally adheres a panty pad upside down.

8.30 p.m. One bottle of white gone, a bottle of red nearly dead, and Belinda, who has been nothing but teary, tired and grumpy since she first fell pregnant in 1987, raises the question that has haunted humankind since the dawn of time – just what use are men? (We started compiling a list over seven years ago, but so far the only things we've written under the title, Things Men Are Useful For are 'hugging' and 'lifting heavy objects'.)

'Actually,' says Heather, 'we have to remove hugging. Apparently Breville or Philips or someone has come up with an appliance that performs that function and you don't have to cook it dinner first'.

8.35 p.m. Leonard knocks. 'Quick, put your clothes on,' I yell to the air as I slowly open the door. Then I lead mouth-agaped Leonard to the throng and call 'Girls! The stripper's here.'

'What?' whispers Leonard, frocked up to the nines in his 'chicks love this' suit. A momentary group-gasp of excitement is followed by an audible choke as the girls lay their eyes upon try-hard Leonard, and Robyn asks, 'Are you a Mormon?'

'Well actually,' says Leonard rather humbly, 'I'm here for urgent advice on women.'

'Oh fabulous,' says Althea, whose life is apparently going to start as soon as she loses 7 kilos. 'Let's get started.'

I warned the girls that anything they said can and would be used against them but, being female, they all agreed that lame Leonard desperately needed nurturing. (How many men does it take to change all twenty-six tyres on a road train? None. You just relax honey, I'll do it.)

'I'm just concerned,' says Leonard, 'that with the new role of females as superwomen men are becoming intimidated, redundant and perhaps obsolete.'

'Well,' says Rosie, 'you know why men today are feeling useless — because that's exactly what they are. Not only did Leonardo da Vinci create countless artistic masterpieces, but he also invented scissors. Nowadays a man has to start a relationship just to get his toilet flushed.'

'Men help with the housework,' Leonard responds.

'Yeah,' says Nici, 'they lift their feet when we're vacuuming.'

'If I were you,' concludes Althea, 'I'd buy shares in Breville or Philips.'

I'm surprised by Leonard's keen involvement in the discussion because, normally, talking to a man is like trying to iron crushed linen.

But then I suddenly saw the situation through Leonard's mind (small space for either sale or rent, rarely used, near new condition) and realised that if need be Leonard would talk about this subject for seventy years, night and day, day and night, because he firmly believed

that somewhere hidden in this room full of women was a
Tub Full of Oil and Mud.

'Time to go, Leonard,' I say hurriedly. 'But first would
you lift something for me?'

start a political movement

or a religion that

worships bikini-line hair

loser

Well, what a week. A spokesperson for pre-pubescent bubble-face Leonardo di Caprio announced the imminent release of 22-year-old Leo's Official Biography. My, how things have changed; in my day it was called a Baby Book.

Oh yes, it's been one of those weeks. Daughter's been in a tizz because Son's stolen her Secret Book. For five days she was worried sick that he might read the contents, but the pressure's off now because she's suddenly remembered that nothing is actually written in it.

And one of those weeks when annual tasks had to be done. You know, those things that come round but once a year: health checks, car rego, cleaning out the vegetable drawer in the fridge. I even did the annual breast check. (But no, I still haven't got any.)

The one thing I couldn't do, however, was renew my car rego because I definitely put my papers somewhere really smart, but for the life of me I couldn't remember where that was.

Of course I could have gone to the Motor Registry for duplicates but I would rather French kiss a fat cow than take a queue ticket at any Motor Registry. One time I went, arrived at 11.30, and there were seven million people waiting before me. I became so desperate I willed other people to die just so

I'd move up the queue faster. (Some of my worst dates have actually died in this way, but they were so boring no one could tell the difference.)

So, rather than take the plunge, I first looked for my rego papers in all the logical places: my glovebox and my receipt file, i.e. my wallet. Then I looked in my sock drawer, where I keep all those things that I have a tendency to lose (e.g. my dignity, self-esteem and pride), and sifted through my cosmetics drawer, where I found my socks.

Then I checked all the places I wouldn't possibly have put the papers in the hope that I might have put them there. I looked in the fridge and I found the iron. (I'd put the iron there to remind me to take the garbage out last Thursday night, but I didn't have time to take the garbage out because I'd spent the whole night looking for the bloody iron.)

Why is it that I can remember the most ridiculous things and I can't remember the important ones? (When a man is described as 'tired and emotional' it means that he is drunk. When a woman is described as 'tired and emotional' it means she's a working mother.)

Some go to great lengths to remember things. I know a tired woman who was so worried she'd forget her own children's names that she renamed them after the circumstances of their conception: Bollinger, Spumante and Oops.

I asked my children if they'd seen my rego papers; perhaps used them to make an aeroplane, or swapped them at school for a crayon? I asked my stoned cleaner if she'd seen my rego papers and she said no, she just had Tally-Hos.

I rang my Mum. She asked if I was sure the papers were lost and if I just hadn't misplaced them. I, of course, found this absolutely enraging until I recalled my Mum thinks a woman can reclaim her lost virginity if she then abstains from sex for the rest of her life. (Note: I'm first in that queue.)

I rang a clairvoyant who had an answering machine, but I didn't leave my number because I figured she could work it out. Then I rang a Psychic Detective who told me 'your papers are in your husband's bedside drawer' – and maybe they will be some time in the future, should I ever get married.

I began to stress, largely because I distinctly remembered putting those papers somewhere odd and thinking, 'I'll remember this place because it's so odd.' I contemplated ringing the Police Rescue Squad.

I rang an emergency therapist but she was in session (as a client), so I finally called one of those 0055 numbers 'for when you're feeling lonely'. Monique told me to 'retrace my steps' since I last saw the papers, so I had two dysfunctional relationships, bought a stove that doesn't work, gained 7 kilos, lost 4, dyed my hair, cut my hair, bought a wig, went to a party with the back of my dress tucked into my undies, and drove to and from the kids' school 984 times.

Then I went to the Motor Registry where I got my new papers in minutes. And while filing them under 'D' for 'don't lose', I came across my other rego papers filed under 'Z' (because that segment had looked so lonely at the time). So I rang Mum to tell her my good news and she said, 'You always find things in the last place you look, maybe next time you should look in the last place first.'

what I did in my holidays

In the holy days I went with my brither and my mum to visit my Aunt Helin. It was fun but not that fun. She does not have a television because she is a lesbian.

Aunty Helin is my mum's sister. I asked Mum where Aunty Helin lives and she said Out Past Bloody Whoop Whoop. That is seven hours away.

Aunty Helin looks like the oldest Bee Gee. She gives us a dollar everytime we see her. And Mum gives us a dollar if we're nice. Sometimes if I'm really nice I charge a dollar-fifty. Mum says this is absorbent. But we don't visit Aunty Helin much because she and Mum had a parting of the waves.

Mum told me Aunty Helin's place was a hole but it is a farm. On the farm she has a house, three horses, two cows and a pig. The house was built by her husband who was also a pig, called Neil, and the horses are also lame ducks.

Neil does not live with Aunty Helin because he makes her sick. Neil is a lazy god-for-nothing son of a bitch and is better off living in some flea-infested bog with some bottle-blonde floozy called Donna.

My bruther says that Donna should live on a farm because Aunty Helin said Donna is a cow.

I have not met Donna or Neil the pig because they are an embracement and her children are ne'er-do-wells, which are wells without water. I have met Aunty Helin's special friend but I am not allowed to talk about her.

Her name is Ellen and she is from New Zealand. So she calls herself Illin. And calls Aunty Helin, Hilin. She sings in a band. The band is called Mona Loud and the Maulers. They do not play anywhere because the socio-political environs of the bush are not condusive to empathetic cohabitation between those of differing sexual preferences. My brither says it's because their music sucks.

Aunty Helin plays the tambourine and she is the only one in time. Mum says this is because she has her own sense of rhythm. Illin says its because Aunty Helin always starts two and a half beats late.

Illin has hair under her arms. Aunty Helin told me Illin is a lesbian. And Mum told me a lesbian is a small type of bird.

On the secind day we went shopping at Coles. Normilly Mum shops at Woolworths, so it was good to compare prices. I found a particularly marked discrepancy between the prices of washing powders for front-loading machines. We bought stuff and then we left.

The next day Mum and Aunty Helin had a heart-to-heart to try to dissolve their differences. My bruther and I weren't supposed to listen and so we shut our eyes. They talked for two ours and got tyred and motional. In the end they revolved to let sleeping logs lie.

On the forth day we did nothing and were not aloud to look bored. Mum says it is good to do nothing sometimes because then you really appreciate it when you have something to do. Mum also thinks Kevin Costner is a very fine actor.

On the fifth day Neil came over and I saw he walks funny. Mum says this is because he spends a lot of time riding horses. But Aunty Helin says it's because he uses the pouch in his Y-fronts as a loose change perse.

On the sixth day Neil said he wanted to be back living with Aunty Helin. Aunty Helin said she couldn't. Because she is a lesbian. Neil said he knew someone. Who knew someone. Who knew of someone. Who thought they were a lesbian. But they did a whole lot of blood tests and discovered she was a diabetic instead.

On the seventh day Neil asked Aunty Helin to give him some money. But she said she wouldn't because Neil would only spend it.

On the atepth day . . . On the ateth day . . . On the last day we said goodbye and Aunty Helin and Illin sang us a song called 'Goodbye'. The words were 'goodbye, goodbye, ahoo goodbye'. And they made us want to leave.

The drive home was very exciting because we saw 12 marsupials on the side of the road. My brither is going to get us into the Guinness Book of Records. A marsupial is a squashed animal.

The drive home took six and a half hours. Because we went from North to South. And that is down hill. My brother vomited.

Next holidays we are going to visit my mother's bruther who is my uncle. He is a cross-dressing fan dancer and also an accountant. He gives very good presents. Last year he gave us all feather dusters and we wore them to Christmas lunch at Grandma's.

The End.

virgin on virginity

Richard Wiggler is telling everyone that I lost my virginity to him. I'm not sure if this is actually true because the first time I had sex was so bad that I don't know if it was the first time I had sex.

I saw my first penis when I was four. It belonged to Angus Nettleton, who was weeing in the garden and I thought he had a small garden hose. The first person who ever tried to see my breasts was the Wonderbra fitter at David Jones. Disappointed at being professionally conquered, she suggested regretfully that my time might be somewhat better spent developing my personality. (I added a zipper to my Wonderbra and now use it as a lovely lace evening bag.)

We learnt about boys at my all-girls school in a subject called Personal Development. We learnt that boys have a Y chromosome and testosterone, and that the overhead projector images of male genitalia are not actual size.

The first boy I held hands with gave me boys' germs. The first boy who loved me called me a bumface. I had my first 'pash' when I was twelve. It was like kissing an octopus pool cleaner. Other intimate physical experiences? Um, nah. Oh yeah, frotting in a train in Spain in 1986; sitting on a heater while wearing flammable undies in 1987; and

giving birth in 1988 after a prolonged and agonised labour.
'Gretel, do you want to go on a drip?'

'#%+!#%^?x#%, you must be joking, that's what got
me here in the first place!'

Suddenly we're allowed to talk about our early sexual
experiences, triggered by that Internet hoax. Oh yes,
'Mark and Dianne, high-school sweethearts' were going to
lose their virginity in the intimacy of the Net.
Pornography? Tragedy? Probably comedy, but either way
denounced as a money-spinning hoax – true to form, it
went before it came.

Nevertheless people are coming out of the woodwork
with tales of the first time they 'did it'. Dinner parties
abound with lurid bullshit about first-time sexual encoun-
ters. It was so romantic, it went on all night, I hung from a
chandelier, he dressed as a Zulu . . . oh sorry, I'm confus-
ing myself with Buttwoman, the porn queen.

I personally don't understand society's obsession with
sex. But maybe I'm doing it wrong. You know, like when
you realise the iron works better if you actually switch it
on. I remember the first time my husband got an erection I
rushed him off to hospital. The last time, and this is going
back years, I called a professional photographer.

The few times I've had sex in my life my partner
thought *rigor mortis* had set in. I was actually trying to be
really sexy by copying a porn video I'd seen at the petrol
station. Well, all right, not the actual video, just the stills
from the back cover.

Sex schmex, who cares? Who on earth has really good
sex and how the hell would they know? There should be

some sort of international gauge like the Richter Scale so we can all see how we're faring. In fact, sex should be acknowledged as the quintessential Olympic sport – epitomising strength, power and endurance, and how to cope when let down by a team member.

But back to Richard Wiggler and me. Well, no sooner had he announced that he'd stolen my girlhood than several rival bidders entered the arena, most of whom I have never met.

The rumours were fantastic. I was irresistible. I'd lost it on mountain tops, in public swimming pools, standing in a queue at Woolworths. I was an absolute bloody legend, the value of my shares started to rise, and there was pressure to divulge the 'doer'. But I needed time to research the facts because virginity is a precious thing and you don't just give it away.

After much deliberation, soul searching and youthful diary reading, e.g. 'Saw Neville today, gawd he's a spunk', I decided I didn't have a clue who my deflowerer was and I would choose from the written submissions: 'We were in love and did it in a motel in Taree. It was fantastic', read Gavin's review. 'We were drunk and I passed out. It was unbelievable' – Felix. 'We did it at recess because she wanted to copy my essay on *Hamlet* ('Hamlet, Man or Moth' – typo). It was the best sex ever' – Enzo.

My God, I thought, I *am* good.

Finally I chose Richard Wiggler, unaware of his specific recollections but recalling that as a teenager he was a real hunk. I called for a meeting to bless him with my decision and realised that now, twenty years later, he is short, fat and gay.

He told me about our alleged encounter: we were watching *The Box*, sex lasted one Copperart ad, and I was an absolute dud.

(Gosh, it really must have been him.)

battle of the sexes

The Dinner Party — *A modern social-realist play about a single woman called Pip and her pathetic efforts to while away a coupled-friend's dinner party by talking to the only other single person in the room, a late-thirties man called Hugh. Without discussing real estate or shares she hopes to maintain his attention without also proffering sex, a rendezvous with a family friend of hers, or some sort of employment opportunity. Other guests may be heard look-at-me laughing while dutifully discussing their labradors, new roller doors, and the funny but tragically pitiful lives of uninvited bores.*

Act 1: Pre-Dinner Drinks

In which Pip meets Hugh and they both wish she had a bigger cleavage.

P: Hi, I'm Pip, you must be Hugh, what do you do?

H: I'm in real estate.

P: Oh. Any hobbies?

H: Yes, I dabble in the stock market.

P: Excuse me, I have to go to the bathroom.

Act 2: Entree and Main Course

In which Pip thoroughly entertains Hugh by passing him the salt.

P: So, tell me, do you have a family?

H: No.

P: No family at all?

H: No.

P: Oh, how fascinating. *(She sculls her wine.)* Are you interested in politics at all?

H: No.

P: Do you have a favourite book?

H: No.

P: Do you have a preferred travel destination?

H: No.

P: Do you have an absolutely hilarious childhood tale?

H: No.

P: Do you perhaps know anyone else's?

H: No.

P: *Parlez-vous Français, Monsieur?*

H: *Non.*

P: Do you have any opinions on this century's greatest living treasure, perhaps – male or female, artist or activist, ascetic or astronaut, politician or poet, polygamist or netball player?

H: No.

P: Do you know that fabulous quote by Steven Wright, 'You can't have everything, where would you put it?'

H: No.

P: So, how do you know the hosts?

H: I don't know.

P: Salt?

H: Yes.

P: Oh what a surprise! Do tell me more.

Act 3: Coffee and Dessert

In which Pip tells a cracker of a joke and Hugh burps.

P: So, how about I tell you all about my kids? . . . I said, how about I tell you all about my kids . . . I said, how about I tell you . . . Oh, sorry, I thought that you'd gone deaf.

H: No, I was dozing.

P: Well, enough about me, let's talk about you. Do you have a preferred outdoor furniture? Were you told that a woman in Kent named her child Depressed Cupboard Cheesecake? Do you use peanut butter as a substitute for shaving foam? Did you hear that Johnny Carson was so naive as a child that he used to sneak behind the barn and do nothing? *(Celine Dion is heard from the stereo in the living room.)* Here, let me guess your star sign: Gemini . . . Leo . . . Virgo . . . Taurus . . . Sagittarius . . . Capricorn . . . Aries . . . Aquarius . . . Scorpio . . . Pisces?

H: Cancer.

P: Yes, I thought so. What about if I told you I once met Madonna? Would you like to meet her? What about if I said I'm rich as rich, my father's Lord Dickdock, my ex-husband's Count Ribald, and my mummy's a compulsive–obsessive psychotic alcoholic who's had so many facelifts her navel is her mouth? Would that make me more interesting?

(Hugh makes a wry grimace.)

P: There we go, is that a smile?

H: No, it's my peptic ulcer.

P: So tell me, Hugh, do you play golf? Have you ever tried singing opera whilst breathing in? *(Dejected pause)* Do you know what's brown and sticky?

H: No.

P: A stick. *(Canned laughter)*

H: *(Burp)*

Act 4: The Farewell

In which our cast bids fond goodbyes and Hugh realises that Pip's bum is nowhere near as enormous as he had at first thought.

H: Goodbye, Pip.

P: Goodbye, Hugh.

H: Lovely to meet you. We must do it again.

P: Most definitely. I've enjoyed my company immensely.

forty-nine ways

Now that 'home-cooked' meals are readily available from the freezer at your local supermarket, it is becoming glaringly obvious that for many of us the challenge of mere existence has passed and life is simply too easy.

No longer required to hunt for food, construct bark shelters, repel marauding beasts or hand-sew our lap-laps with sabre-tooth needles, we find ourselves leading modern lives that are vacuous, repetitive, without risk, and fundamentally unstimulating. Hence the emergence of The Advencha Holiday.

Now, whereas many might consider the words 'adventure' and 'holiday' to be mutually exclusive (rather like semi-permanent), apparently this is not the case. Filling one with adrenalin hitherto undiscovered, Advencha Holidays allegedly make one feel more alive by testing one's willpower, physical strength and bowel vulnerability.

In my day 'confronting death' meant sharing Christmas lunch with your relatives, but in this whirlybird, fast-paced world in which we live, simply enduring Aunty Meg's breath is no longer enough. Starting with the Running of the Bulls, Advencha escapades have expanded into bungee jumping while riding a bicycle (I kid you not), oxygenless, one-legged climbing of Mount Everest and, in the US, voluntary internment in a maximum security jail. Fabulous stuff, there's no doubt about it, but unfortunately skewed towards the rich.

But wait, there is hope. Because, recognising that not everyone can afford the luxury of a well-kitted and catered near-death experience, yet wanting to make this phenomenon accessible to all, I have created a list of activities one may pursue within the limitations of one's personal budget and lifestyle – activities which provide the quintessential characteristics of any Advencha Holiday: pain, suffering, fear and discomfort.

Forty-nine Ways To Make Your Life More Difficult

1 Fall in love . . . with a loser. (Writer's note: names and numbers available on request.)
2 Wear your G-string backwards.
3 Only take every second breath.
4 Go skiing without skis.
5 Park in a clearway.
6 Floss over-vigorously.
7 Walk dog poo through your house.
8 Wear your shoes on the wrong feet.
9 Get married.
10 Get divorced.
11 Get married, have children, get divorced.
12 Just have children.
13 Neglect to remove coat-hangers before you put your clothes on.
14 Spread scandalous rumours about yourself.

15 Catch up with an old boyfriend. Hear him talk about how attractive you used to be.

16 Hop everywhere.

17 Go through doorways without opening the doors.

18 Play golf in an electrical storm using only irons.

19 Hire tradesmen then wait for their arrival.

20 Try to make rhythmical love while listening to Thelonius Monk.

21 Speak while the footy's on.

22 Go to dinner with an ex and his new girlfriend. Listen to them talk about their happiness.

23 Befriend your ex-boyfriend's new girlfriend.

24 Watch the director's cut of *Titanic*. Try to guess the ending.

25 Run out of toilet paper.

26 Drink Sydney water.

27 Cover your body in chips and food scraps and lie amongst a plague of seagulls.

28 Have sex with Bill Clinton.

29 Try not to have sex with Bill Clinton.

30 See the glass as empty.

31 Wear a full body cast. And go dancing.

32 Wear local anaesthetic as lip balm.

33 Try to read James Joyce.

34 Take a farting dog for a long family drive.

35 Date a mime artist.

36 Have sex with a mime artist.

37 Attend an Andrew Lloyd Webber musical.

38 Speak in tongues (without the assistance of either drugs or alcohol).

39 Wear *lederhosen* whilst horse-riding.

40 Apply lipstick whilst horse-riding.

41 Play tennis with a spoon.

42 Become an obsessive–compulsive; leave your house
    with the iron on.

43 Try to do your kid's homework.

44 Endeavour to lip-read SBS TV.

45 Pluck your bikini line.

46 Attempt to justify your existence to your god.

47 Attempt to justify your existence to your mother.

48 Cut your fingernails too close to the skin.

49 Go off your medication.

relationship rewind

I hugged and kissed the children goodbye. 'Be good, brush your teeth, and I'll see you in three days.'

'I'll always remember you,' said seven-year-old Eppie.

'Hope your plane doesn't crash and you die,' said Zeke.

Well, the plane did crash, but I didn't die. No, I bobbed around in the Pacific for several hours, watching my life flash before my eyes, and trying to tune into someone else's. Luckily I hadn't touched a meal during the flight, because those who had sank like stones.

I was finally rescued by a very attractive coastguard, who'd been alerted to my frenzied life-jacket-plastic-whistle-blowing by a bionic dog in Alaska. I was then heli-coptered to an oil rig where I organised an agent and was immediately interviewed by a women's weekly magazine and the commercial TV station Channel Sevine. The jour-nalists were lovely and very professional, encouraging me to embellish my story to ensure its film potential. They waited patiently as I acted on their advice (had a complete makeover, fell in love with my rescuer and had my heart broken on discovering he was gay), then gave me a ride to the passing cruise ship, *Fairgo*. From here I planned to disembark at my original destination, the legendary Hyperbole Isle; however, whilst frolicking on the deck,

I chanced to jump overboard and ended up in the sea again.

I jumped overboard at around 3 p.m. whilst watching some blond people playing quoits. All was going fabulously until one woman, a tizzy-haired rather gammy-looking thing in too-short shorts took a particularly amateurish throw, hurled the quoit overboard, forgot to let go and as a consequence went over the ship's rail. She was followed by her boyfriend, who leapt overboard to rescue her. And they were followed by yours truly because I have always been a follower.

Still wearing the life jacket from my aeroplane adventure (because I actually found it rather figure flattering) I floated to a deserted island paradise. From there I sadly watched the tizzy-haired blonde woman sink below the water's surface while her breasts floated to the horizon, where I understand they later became a small independent nation.

'Sob sob sob.'

'My goodness,' I thought. 'That sounds like Grimwilly Tremwith.'

'Sob sob sob, snort!'

'Good grief,' I thought. 'It is!'

And sure enough distraught upon the sands beside me was bubble-tits' boyfriend, and the former love of my life, Grimwilly Of-Course-I-Love-You-I'm-Here-Aren't-I Tremwith.

'Hello, Grimwilly,' I said, in Dulux cool tones, having never truly forgiven him for justifying having sex with the caterer at our engagement party on the grounds that he was cold.

'Hi, Babe,' replied Grimwilly, semi-conscious.

'No, Babe's floated away. I'm Darling,' I replied.

'But . . . where am I?' he asked.

'You've died, Grimwilly,' I responded, 'and you've gone to Heaven.'

'But what are you doing here?' he said.

'Well, turns out I'm God.'

'Jesus,' gulped Grimwilly.

'No, God,' I replied. 'And as such it falleth upon me to determine whether you should stay here in heaven or burn for all eternity. So confess your sins.'

'Um,' stuttered Grimwilly. 'My life has been full of lies and deception. I don't really need an hour on the toilet, I'm not allergic to the vacuum cleaner, I often said you looked great in outfits that actually made you look like a beanbag, and the budgie wasn't the farter in our family, it was me!'

Grimwilly continued: 'But the biggest sin of all is that I never let you know how wonderful, beautiful and smart you really are. I hid my adoration because, like many men, I am intimidated by the strength of the modern woman and feel I can only truly assert my masculinity by undermining your career, intelligence, self-worth and goals. I'm sorry, Darling. I love you.'

'Oh, go to hell,' I said.

And with that I was rescued by my coastguard again.

'Guess what, I'm not gay any more,' he bellowed, hauling me to his chopper with his toes, 'I love you and respect your mind, strength and career.'

'That's nice,' I replied. 'But, more importantly, do you think this life jacket makes me look like a beanbag?'

olden daze

My children ask me what my life was like ten years ago, in the olden days, i.e. before they were born. Well, I remember what it was like when I was my children's age, what it was like to be safe walking to school, what it was like to eat real fruit, what it was like to be in love with your first-aid teacher and volunteer as the victim in need of mouth-to-mouth, lie on the floor, and call to the instructor, 'Do it to me, baby, I'm yours'.

But do I remember what my life was like ten years ago? I'm not sure.

As someone who had their first mid-life crisis at the age of three I can tell you it's not an easy question to answer. You know, I sometimes imagine that my best years are behind me and regret that I didn't make the most of them. I never learnt the piano, failed to recognise true love, neglected to make the most of my okay breasts before they wandered off to meet my navel.

But the reality is I don't recall what my life was like ten years ago because it was just about then that the forgetful hormones kicked in along with the fluid retention, and I became pregnant with my first child.

Nowadays pregnancy is *haute couture*; in my day it certainly wasn't. Today pregnancy is the ultimate fashion accessory, so cool you can't co-host a game show without it. When I was first pregnant and appearing on an evening current affairs show I was broadcast only from the neck up, under the well-researched scientific premise that 'pregnancy would put people off their dinner'.

Ten years ago you could sack a woman when she got 'knocked up', and males could tell a fellow employee that they liked her pregnant because 'it made her tits so huge'. (Ironically enough, ten years later, those commentators probably have breasts bigger than mine.)

Oh! So *there's* a change. Ten years ago I had bigger breasts. (I know I go on and on about my mammaries but, for heaven's sake, somebody's got to.) I am also pretty certain that ten years ago I thought the Fallopian Tubes would make a great name for band and I thought a urethra was a famous black soul singer from the seventies. But what was my life like? Well, I don't know.

Ten years ago, I believe, I was sexually active. Today I have the sex drive of a tricycle. I have huge dark circles under my eyes and a look that's permanently fixed upon my face that says, 'No, it isn't funny, it's dangerous'. To make myself at all attractive to men I have to dress up as a golf bag.

Ten years ago I had never even held a baby and had been known to look up the cooking time for a three-minute egg. Ten years ago the only people I knew who used the phrases 'Sit down and be quiet' and 'Just do as you're told' worked in Kings Cross on Saturday nights dressed as whip-carrying nurses and nuns.

Three thousand, six hundred and fifty days ago I had

never kissed someone and then had them vomit on me. (Oh, actually I had – a charming ex-boyfriend who answered to the nickname 'mange brain' and whose current wife I understand is suing his manhood for fraud and misrepresentation.)

Ten years ago I remember telling my husband I was going to be sick in the car and he gave me my clutch bag to throw up in. Ten years ago I realised that should your obstetrician take an urgent phone call mid-internal examination, it is more than likely his daughter Phoebe ringing from pony camp to ask for more pocket money. Ten years ago my partner reminded me to breathe during the labour, advice I personally believe should be saved for that special time after the birth when you get your doctor's bill.

Ten years ago I thought a partner could 'share the birthing experience', not realising that what this actually means is he talks footy with the doctor throughout the labour, then as the baby emerges snaps lurid photos which ensure his workmates can never again look you in the eye. (Years later I submitted these photos to a lovely motherhood quest. P.S. I did not win.)

Yep, ten years ago, I was ripped, torn, tortured and tested, then finally confronted by a little red screaming face that said, 'Please look after me, I'm absolutely helpless'. And I said, 'Not now dear, I've just had a baby'.

So that's what happened ten years ago-ish. I became a mother and learnt that motherhood is like passing a camel through the eye of a needle and then looking after it for the rest of your life.

But regarding the question, what was my life like

before that, in the olden days? I honestly haven't a clue. I suspect it was full of sleep and self-indulgence but postnatal forgetfulness happens to all women. God planned it specially that way.

sweat dreams

Last week Dana dreamt she had wings and was flying through a storm, Peter dreamt he was a raging lion biting through his cage, Anton dreamt he was a bloodied soldier proudly fighting with no limbs, and I dreamt I fixed the vacuum cleaner by removing a ball of hairy Blu-Tack from the nozzle.

Dana said my dream was pathetic. When you're in a four-day dream-analysis forum, she said, you have to let go of your wake-time existence and explore the significance of the subconscious. Well, sorry Winged Storm-flyer, fab dreams are not my thing, I mean it's not like I don't want to dream about being a man-eating dragon, it's just that I don't.

I can't even get reception on the corniest dream cliches – last time I tried to have sex with the Chippendales I dreamt I was ironing their G-strings.

Dana said I didn't try hard enough. I said you shouldn't have to try because trying necessitates the intrusion of the conscious into the subconscious, therefore negating the intrinsic purity of any dreamtime discovery. Dana said eat a spicy dinner, that'll make you dream. That night I ate a spicy dinner and dreamt I had the runs.

'You dreamt you had diarrhoea!' whispered appalled

Dana, just prior to announcing that she had dreamt she was a lesbian warrior boiling happy snakes in a pot of beer and pizza.

'How could you tell people you dreamt you had the squits?' she demanded. 'Even dullard Peter dreamt he went to school with no pants on and had sex with his lunch.'

'I'm sorry,' I replied. 'I'll try to do better.'

That night I borrowed from a friend's porn library and fell asleep watching *Bride's Bed Revisited*. I watched the rumpy humpty dumpty, marvelled at how much money there is in the porn industry, and then dreamt I was an accountant.

'Don't you dare tell anyone!' said Dana, the next day. 'No man is ever going to find you at all enticing with a sick subconscious like that.' (Oh yes, I forgot, the motivation for our spiritual dream forum attendance was essentially to pick up blokes. Having concluded that all conscious men are repressed as a result of environmental conditioning, we'd decided to communicate with the male subconscious in search of a virgin pure essence.)

By the start of the third day, as we sat on beanbags trying not to fart after a big breakfast of date muffins, it was painfully clear that the blokes wanted Dana with her night-time mental meanderings and this riled me to the core.

One, because I hate to lose and, two, because I think Dana cheated by plagiarising from *The Happy Hooker*.

Obviously I needed professional assistance, so that night I rang Gorgeous Bod Jim, an old boyfriend who used to drive me insane by reciting his dreams *ad* bloody *nauseam*. 'Hi,' I said, feeling a twinge in my heart at the memory of just how hard and long we'd tried to make our relationship work. 'Had any good dreams lately, Jimbo?' And off he went, regaling me with his noddy-land shenanigans while I memorised every word.

The following morning, dressed in traditional Amish clothing to highlight the juxtaposition between my former austere self and the new beguiling devil within, I prepared to win the boys' hearts with my borrowed night-time adventures.

Peter began the session and said he'd dreamt of meeting an angel who looked just like Dana. Anton followed and said he'd married a goddess whose name was Dana and they raised children who were rays of sunshine. Dana said she dreamt she fell in love with two bananas and they gave her a permanent inner-city parking space. And then, of course, it was my turn.

No one was interested so I started with the simple phrase, 'I was nude'. Then I spoke of magical lighting, fabulous costumes, amazing music, exceptional dancing, pythons, aftershave and depilatory.

'Fantastic,' said Dana.

'Any tunnels?' asked Pete.

'No, just trains,' I replied.

'Any scoops of ice-cream, mountains or hills, or anything at all resembling breasts?'

'No,' I replied. 'Just a warehouse interior, but it was fabulously designed.'

I waited for an interpretation and the boys' subsequent adoration.

'Gretel, I'm sorry,' said Anton solemnly. 'Fabulous

dream, we all agree, but it says you're a latent homosexual male.'

(Gee, thanks a lot, Gorgeous Bod James – no wonder our relationship failed.)

Then the three of them left for beer and pizza.

tooth decay

Frightening, scary,
really spooky,
going to the dentist.

The receptionist has perfect teeth. They're white and
even and obviously flossed after every single meal. It's
been seven months since my last dental visit and the first
time I flossed was this morning. I wish the receptionist
would cover up her mouth with the funky sunglasses I
see sitting on her desk. I bet her breath smells like
Impulse.

She's smiling at me to try and make me smile back. How
unbelievably rude! I want to tell her I'm sick and that I
have to go home. If I had false teeth I could just post them.
Or take a photo and then send a fax. I can't believe that
science can create a sheep from a single cell yet I still have
to take my own teeth to the dentist!

What's happened to the world's priorities? If everyone
hates going to the dentist so much, at least the soothing,
calming gas could be administered in the waiting room.
(But then again, why bother when perusing the waiting
room's collection of ten-year-old women's mags will just as
effectively anaesthetise the brain?)

Tick, tick, tick. It's nearly my turn. I run to the toilets to ring from my mobile and say there's a bomb in the building. I dial quickly, get put on hold, and hear a tap tap tap on the cubicle. It's the dental assistant, she has perfect teeth and enormous breasts. What a waste, why have both!? 'The dentist is ready for you now,' she says.

Oh, right, howdy doody then, wouldn't want to keep him waiting. (He's a new dentist. I was expelled from my last.)

I'm ushered into the surgery by Big Bosoms, who asks me how I am today, then walks off to another room as I answer. I'm left quite alone in the white, white surgery with all the dentist's weapons. Pokey things. Shiny things. Very, very sharp things. I try to bundle the really danger-ous ones into my shoulder-bag but The Dentist enters the room to the theme music from *Jaws*.

I think The Dentist says hello but it is possibly 'Bloody hell. Get a load of your teeth'. It's hard to understand verbal communication with someone who is wearing the sort of head-to-toe protective clothing that one would normally expect to find on an anally retentive beekeeper.

I'm seated, bibbed, electronically reclined and then, as soon as my clamp-opened mouth is chock-a-block with pointy, sharp, metallic things, The Dentist asks, 'So what have you been doing lately?'

He's searching for cavities and humming off-key. He sighs, he stops, he starts again; obviously surveying the tragic terrain of my teeth is exhausting and difficult. He asks if I floss. I say yes, twice a day. Why do I lie to my dentist? Don't know. Same reason that I memorise all the eye charts before I go and visit the optometrist.

I hate this beekeeper, and, as he probes with all the finesse of someone who's knitting while on a trotting horse, I imagine wooing his fingers into my mouth and then biting his entire hand off.

Open wider, he says. Oh okay, wait a second, I'll just undo the zip in the back of my head. This is worse than giving birth!

Big Bosoms plays a Swedish pop CD and I think I'm going to throw up. I hate you all, I gurgle to myself 'til they insert a vacuum cleaner into my mouth and try to suck my tongue out.

'Are you all right?' inquires The Dentist as he approaches with what appears to be a Whipper Snipper and I instinctively reach for his testicles.

'Are you all right?' he repeats quickly. Compared to what, I wonder? That performance artist who hangs himself from the ceiling with huge fish hooks inserted through his flesh? No, I'm not.

I want my mother. I mean, who is this guy anyway? This is the most intimate moment I've had in eight years and I don't even know the fellow's star sign. 'Do you like ferrets?' I inquire.

'We need gas,' he says to Big Bosoms.

I breathe in so deeply that parts of Africa begin to submerge, but still *compos mentis*, I breathe in again and again . . . and again . . . and . . . then the lovely Swedish dentist starts to sing and we all float down the spittle plughole to a land where all is white and very straight and we're happy and we laugh. Aha ha ha ha ha.

The dentist finishes and suggests I leave but I want to

live in the chair. They pinch my face, force-feed me oxygen,
but still, I am in dental love zone.

Give her something.

Bang she's conscious;

dental bills do that every time.

you will never be number one

in the life of any man who

has a nickname for his willy

quote quota

A lot of people nowadays are turning to instruction books for assistance with their lives. Colourful books of wisdom, compiled by bearded people, have become the bibles of the nineties and abound on the best-seller lists. I myself confess to having consumed these life-recipe books, indeed I was the first in the queue for the US release *Forget Money, Work For Your Soul*, but went off the author when the sequel, *How To Make Money From Your Soulful Existence*, came out.

Even as a child, when lost or confused I sought strength and guidance from the words of others. Initially, like most children, I misguidedly sought succour from my mother, whose life-deterring words still ring in my ears: 'You think your life's bad, why don't you take a look at mine!'

My schooling provided little bits of information that have never been of use (e.g. did you know Not Able To Fornicate was the name of a Native American?), and my father read me only one thing of life import, and that was by analogical accident: 'Have you ever noticed how, in all books, people coming into a room always gently close the door behind them? I suppose the reason for this is that if they closed the door in front of themselves they'd still be outside.' (Lennie Lower)

And so it came to be that at the age of nine I began my

own life-affirming book, which is still a work in progress (rather like the well-arts-funded modern sculpture in our local park – a mound of choreographed garbage bins, nick-named Waiting for Otto). This collection of quips has inspired, comforted, or amused me even through the dark-est years of my life (in particular 1974–78 when my mother kept getting my hair cut like a coconut). May they doeth the sameth for thee.

Life Lines

1 Pubic hair is no substitute for wit. *J. B. Priestley*
2 Canberra, one of the world's most exciting cities. *Canberra tourism brochure*
3 Tell me, was it you or your brother who was killed in the war? *Rev. W. A. Spooner*
4 You are going to call him 'William'? What kind of name is that? Every Tom, Dick and Harry is called William. Why don't you call him Bill? *Samuel Goldwyn*
5 All you need in life is ignorance and confidence and then success is sure. *Mark Twain*
6 Very nice, though there are dull stretches. *Antoine de Rivarol (reviewing a two-line poem)*
7 My life needs editing. *Mort Sahl*
8 The play was a great success, but the audience was a failure. *Oscar Wilde*
9 Not a shred of evidence exists in favour of the idea that life is serious. *Brendan Gill*
10 My life has no purpose, no direction, no aim, no meaning and yet I'm happy. I can't figure it out. What am I doing right? *Charles M. Schulz*

11 To be good is noble, but to teach others how to be good is nobler, and less trouble. *Mark Twain*

12 You know there's something about me that makes a lot of people want to throw up. *Pat Boone*

13 Formula for success. Rise early, work hard, strike oil. *J. Paul Getty*

14 Millions long for immortality who do not know what to do with themselves on a rainy Sunday afternoon. *Susan Ertz*

15 Sometimes the male praying mantis continues to copulate even after the female has bitten off his head and part of his upper torso. Typical. *Aunty Margie*

16 In baiting a mouse-trap with cheese, always leave room for the mouse. *Saki*

17 New and stirring things are belittled because if they are not belittled the humiliating question arises, 'Why then are you not taking part in them?'. *H. G. Wells*

18 Of all the thirty-six alternatives, running away is best. *Chinese proverb*

19 May your left ear wither and fall into your right pocket. *Arab curse*

20 A rich man's joke is always funny. *Thomas Brown*

21 Rembrandt is not to be compared in the painting of character with our extraordinarily gifted English artist Mr Rippingille. *John Hunt*

22 After we made love he took a piece of chalk and made an outline of my body. *Joan Rivers*

23 Show me a good loser and I'll show you a loser. *Anon*

24 There ain't no rules here! We're trying to accomplish something. *Thomas Edison*

25 After twelve years of therapy my psychiatrist said
   something that brought tears to my eyes. He said, 'No
   hablo inglis'. *Ronnie Shakes*
26 May you live all the days of your life. *Jonathan Swift*

la petite princess

The story so far: It's Friday evening and my seven-year-old daughter has a little schoolfriend over to stay the night. The schoolfriend's name is Pixie. She only eats ham-and-pineapple pizza, is allowed to watch seven hours of TV every night, never goes to bed until after midnight, and sometimes doesn't even go to bed at all! Her grandparents are ghosts, her mother is a princess, and her father is the most important brain surgeon in Australia and once got paid ONE HUNDRED DOLLARS!

By 8 p.m. after consuming seven-eighths of a family-sized ham-and-pineapple pizza, Pixie announces that she feels really sick and has decided that she wants to go home.

'Well,' I say, 'let's ring your parents and we'll see what they think.'

I ask my daughter what she did with Pixie's phone number and my daughter says my son took it. My son and I know this is entirely probable. Ever since he made me a cup of tea by squeezing the teabags down the kettle nozzle then adding the water and boiling the lot, he and I both know anything is possible (except, of course, removing the tea bags from the kettle).

After much interrogation I get nothing from my son,

despite the fact that this being October it is now officially the time when parents can start bribing their kids with lavish promises of bountiful gifts or, alternatively, terrifying Christmas threats of absolute presentlessness.

So, remembering we once lost two frogs, a white mouse, and a rather attractive plumber in the same manner (where is he/she/it/they? I don't know but I think my brother/sister took it), I abandon all hope of finding the note and ask Pixie if she knows her own phone number.

'Yes,' replies Pixie quite confidently, '9-4-7-6-4-2-1-5-4-4-3-2-8-9-9-6.'

'Well, what's your daddy's name?' I ask, hoping to find the number in the *White Pages*.

'Bruce,' she immediately replies.

'Is he in the phone book?' I ask her gently.

'No, he's in the gaol,' she says.

'Why's he in gaol?' I enquire, aghast.

'Because he played too much golf.'

'Maybe your mum's in the book', I say. 'Do you perhaps know her last name?'

'No, but I know my stepdad's.'

'Oh good, what is it?' I ask excitedly.

'Pallyspiariousouskoofa,' Pixie replies.

'Can you spell that?' I ask.

'No, but he can.'

'Are you sure you really want to go home?' I say. 'We could watch a video instead.'

'I've seen every video,' she replies. (Well, of course she has, as would anyone else whose pony cost $20,000, whose brother was kidnapped before he was born, and whose next-door neighbour is Scary Spice, sssssssshhhhh, Mummy said not to tell anybody).

Now my daughter begins to cry.

'What's the matter?' I say, concerned she's being scarred by her little guest's sudden and urgent wish to leave.

'How come Pixie's seen every video?' she sobs.

Time to take Pixie home. 'Do you know where you live?'

'Yes,' says Pixie. 'Sydney, Australia.'

'Do you know your address?'

'I'm hungry.'

'I thought you felt sick.'

'I feel sick 'cause I'm hungry.'

'Well, perhaps you should go to sleep then.'

'My grandma felt sick exactly like this . . . and then she died.' (Oh yeah, sick schmick, who was your grandma, Joan of Arc?) Now all three children start to cry and I resolve to forbid my normally happy offspring to socialise ever again, for the rest of their lives.

After much discussion the children reassure me that they all know how to get to Pixie's house because she lives just near the school and 'everyone knows where she lives'. And so we head off in the car, in the dark, but before we even get to the end of the street, the children all fall fast asleep, So I reverse, park and carry them one by one back inside our house.

In the morning, Pixie's father arrives to take her home.

'How did everything go?' the dillionaire husband of a princess and stepfather of a fairy asks.

'Oh great, bed at midnight, seven hours of TV, the usual family-sized ham-and-pineapple pizza for breakfast.'

'Oh no!' he gasps. 'She's allergic to ham-and-pineapple pizza. You know, her grandmother died from eating one!'

Ooooops.

hello?

'Hello and thank you for calling God in Heaven. Unfortunately all lines are currently busy but your call is important to us so please hold for the first available operator.' I hold and listen to 'Greensleeves'.

'Thank you for holding. Your call has been placed in a queue and will be answered shortly.' 'Greensleeves' turns into 'Tie a Yellow Ribbon' played on a xylophone and I wonder if I've perhaps accidentally rung Hell.

'Tie a yellow ribbon round the old . . . Thank you for holding. Your call has moved up in the queue and will be answered as soon as possible. By the way, have you thought about investing in After-Life Insurance? Feel free to ask about our no-obligation free quote.' I continue to hold the line, and listen to an *a cappella* group. The Four Hoarse Men sing 'Hey Jude'.

'We apologise for the delay. Did you know that at Coles this week sausages are only 79 cents a kilo! Hello and thank you for calling God in Heaven. If you have a superannuation query please press one, now. For account enquiries, please press two; for account payments, please press three; for information regarding Elvis, please press four; for travel advice, please press five. For all other queries, please stay on the line. To hear the complete selection again, please press six.'

I press six just to be sure since you don't want to be a time-wasting imbecile when you're ringing Heaven because if anyone can chase a prank call, it's God. (Hello God, is Fred Wall there? Is John Wall There? Is Simon Wall there? Are any walls there? Well, what's holding your house up! Boom Boom.)

'Hello and thank you for calling God in Heaven. If you have a superannuation query, please press one, now. For account enquiries, please press two; for account payments, please press . . .' I actually want to ask God a question, so I hold the line and wait for some angel to answer. I listen to a version of 'What's New Pussycat' in which Tom Jones has been replaced by a harp.

'Hello. Please enter your account number.'

'Oh no, I'm sorry, I'm waiting to speak to . . .'

'Please enter your account number.'

I press six to get back to the selection.

'I'm sorry, your number was incomplete. Please try again.'

I press six again, and again. Three times in total.

'Thank you, Lucifer. Your credit account is . . . over-drawn, if you . . .'

I hang up.

Dejected I sit and wonder how in Heaven's name I can get through to God. With the amount of time it appears I'm going to have to hang on the phone I'd be quicker just waiting to meet Him/Her in person. But I have a question that has consumed me for more than fifteen years and I really want to know the answer right now. I've asked mere mortals over and over but not one of them has shed light on my query.

And now my children are growing older and soon

they'll want to know the answer, and if I can give them nothing else in this life, I would like to give them this.

I wonder who on earth can help me make contact with the big guy. I must know someone who knows someone who slept with someone who knows God.

Nah!

What about someone who went to school with Mary Magdalene, or perhaps played rugby with St Peter or the Apostles? Who do I know who's Heaven-connected?

Of course! Australia's very own omnipresence, the one and only Ray Martin. I call him on his shoe phone. He's having his hair done, but he can still talk. 'Yes,' he says. 'I know Goddo. He's a good bloke.' Turns out Ray and God first met on *The Midday Show* and have played golf regularly ever since. Ray gives me God's mobile number. I dial and get straight through.

'Hello, God speaking.' (His voice is much higher than I imagined, he sounds a bit like a jockey.)

'Hello, God,' I say. 'It's Gretel Killeen here.'

'Ah yes,' he says. 'Has the rash cleared up?' (Good heavens, he is all-knowing.)

'Yes, thank you. God, can I ask you something? I have an all-consuming question that has prevented me fully grasping the notion that everything has a reason.'

'Yes, my child, I am all-knowing, please asketh *moi*.'

I am scared and trembling, my mouth is dry, but I summon all my nerves and strength and say, 'Excuse me, God, but I was just wondering why cyclists wear those silly tight shorts.'

'I haven't a clue,' God replies.

ma doona

Has anyone ever died trying to put a doona cover on?

On Wednesday evening I started to put the fluffy, white, queen-sized doona back inside the freshly washed and sunshine-dried olive-green doona cover.

On Thursday morning the kids filed a missing persons report. On Thursday evening friends and relatives put out a search party.

On Friday morning the cleaning lady heard muffled screams emanating from my bedroom. On Friday evening Police Rescue retrieved me.

On Saturday morning the doctor announced I needed a day of rest. By Saturday afternoon my children had decided this meant we should go fishing. I organised a bountiful feast, reels, bait, sunblock, jackets and hats while the children sat on the couch.

I rang Davo for assistance. He'd often spoken of his harbour-moored boat and I thought his involvement could make our outing even more delightful. Despite his raging hangover Davo agreed with enthusiasm. I realise, in retrospect, that he was still drunk.

We arranged to meet Davo at the jetty. I rested as the children and I played 'I'm starving – what's there to eat – yuk, I hate that' until Davo arrived 50 minutes late, looked me straight in the eye and said, 'Gee you looked tired. You know, you should relax.'

The sea was blue,
The sky was clear,
The sun shone o'er water.
As I launched Davo's 12-foot aluminium dinghy for my
son and daughter.

(And Davo lay snoring on the beach.)

'All aboard!' I gasped.

'Where's Davo's speedboat?'

'This is it.'

'Oh MU-U-UM!'

The sea was calm,
The sun was warm,
The sky was azure blue,
'Could you start the engine please, Dave,' I said.
'No I can't,' said Dave, 'I'm gonna spew.'

Oh gross!' said the kids. 'Can we go home now?'

'No,' I said, smiling firmly. 'We are going to stay here and fish, and what's more we are going to enjoy it.'

So we sat there with our handreels cast, doing nothing, as the saying goes, but teaching our worms to swim.

The sun was getting pretty warm,
Our skin began to burn,
I heard waves lap upon the shore,
And then I heard, 'I'm boooooooooooooooooooooored.'
'Be quiet,' I said, 'you'll scare the fish.'

'There aren't any fish here!' said the kids. I asked Davo for his verdict on the matter but he said nothing because he was unconscious.

'Lana Pate's mother caught seventy-two fish with a single prawn.'

'Nichola Federson's dad caught 309 fish in a boat once and he was just trying to wee over the side.'

We floated there
Without a bite
No sign of fish for fishin'
It was bearable 'til Davo moaned,
'I wish this boat had a television'.

'Mu-u-um,' whinged the kids, 'why aren't there any fish?' And all of a sudden there was a tug on my line and I hauled in a John Dory that was so bloody huge the sea level lowered when I bucketed it.

'Yeah, Mummy!' squealed my adorable children as we bobbed atop the gentle sea under the warm caressing rays of the sun.

'Mummy's the best, Mummy's the greatest. We love youuuuuuuu.'

Oh, we laughed and sang. Then we kissed the fish, hugged the fish, christened it John John Dory and prepared to throw it back.

The sun was really stinking hot,
The wee boat smelt like vomit,
The kids began to hate their Mummy.
'Cause I could not get that bloody hook
out of the fish's tummy.

(The fish had swallowed it hook, line and sinker.)

'We're going to have to kill him,' I said.

'Noooo!' screamed the kids.

'I have to,' I said. 'It's the kindest thing to do.'

'Noooo!' screamed the kids.

'I'll kill it quickly. I'll put it out of its misery. I promise it won't feel a thing.'

'Murderer,' my children softly whispered. Then we solemnly buried John John Dory at sea and started the short journey back.

The kids and I cried the whole drive home,
And no one spake a word,
Except Davo who spoke of a pub and a schooner,
But I didn't listen, because I was dreaming
of relaxing inside my doona.

irresistible *moi*

Friday

- High-profile ad agency rings out of the blue, scouting for a face to promote a brand new fragrance. They wonder if I'm interested. The fragrance makes a woman healthy, irresistible and very sporty – in a similar way to all feminine hygiene products.
- Searched the house for 'irresistible' photo. Found only my baby portrait, in which the photographer apparently found me so irresistible he made me lie *under* the bearskin rug.

Saturday

- Spent morning watching son play cricket. Tried to imagine a more boring sport, remembered hearing tale of former Australian cricket captain lying on his death bed. His life flashed before his eyes . . . and he fell asleep.
- Resolved to make suggestion to the Cricket Board that the game be reduced to two 15-minute halves.
- Went grocery shopping in the afternoon at our local mall. Saw cheerful Christmas decorations. Became depressed. Couldn't bear the thought of the next six weeks – being confronted by fake snow, reindeer, bells and tinsel every time I bought meat and vegies. Had

irresistible photo taken with Santa. I looked disgusting but the chops looked good.

- Rang Mum. 'I always look terrible in photos,' I said. 'Yes, dear, I know,' she replied.

Sunday

- Went to barbie with my kids, my friends (Rob Sausage and Jane Sausage), and Rob and Jane's kids (Sausage Junior and Little Sausage). My kids were suspiciously well behaved. Rob and Jane's kids were shy and dysfunctional – suspect this is because of their surname, Sausage.

Monday

- Rang model agency friend to get name of professional photographer for my irresistible portrait. She suggested two – one specialising in special effects, the other in still life.
- Booked session with photographer. Spent two hours doing my hair and make-up. Arrived at photographer's to hear him say, 'Hi, I'll take you first to the dressing-room so you can do your hair and make-up.'
- Lots of photos eventually taken of me wearing brave face.

Tuesday

- MC'd award lunch. Interpreter for the deaf standing on stage translated every speaker – except me.
- After the ceremony, hailed a cab, got inside, and the vacant sign stayed up.
- Got home and received fan letter from eight-year-old girl. 'Dear Greta Killem, I have just finished reading your book *Cherry Pie*. What was it about?'
- Cooked dinner for kids, they said it was fabulous. 'This

fish is great!' they exclaimed with glee. Pity it was chicken.

Wednesday

- Asked by brainstorming group to suggest potential sponsors for Olympic events. Could only think of Viagra possibly sponsoring the pole vaulting.
- Received photos. Looked vomit-inducing. Could not believe I paid a professional photographer an absolute fortune and still only looked like myself!

Thursday

- Crispin rang and said, 'Did you know there's a company in Australia called Schindler's Lifts?'
- Asked Davo if he knew someone who could photograph me looking irresistible. He said he'd paint my portrait instead. Asked him when he'd like me to sit for him. No sittings, he said, too distracting. He wanted to paint my essence.
- Two hours later, painting of barbecued prawn arrived. Apparently Davo painted my essence while watching a cooking show.
- Finally, desperate, took kids for walk in park so they could casually photograph the irresistible *moi*. (Told them on way home that Mr Whippy only plays 'Fur Elise' when he's run out of ice-cream.)

Thursday afternoon

- Read tabloid newspaper article in which all potentially offensive dialogue was apparently neutered by the editor's removal of every letter but the first. Reminded me of my favourite joke:
Knock knock.

Who's there?

F . . .

F . . . who?

F . . . whom.

- Got kids' photos back from chemist. Best shots ever taken of me, the most fabulous I've ever looked.

- Submitted photos to ad agency.

Friday

- Got job for 'irresistible woman' fragrance. As the 'before' shot.

fairy tales

Once upon a time there was a very nice aunt. She wasn't rich, because some ne'er-do-well had taken a vast amount of her money, and she wasn't beautiful, because she hadn't slept for more than eleven years (since the birth of her first child), but she had a good and kind heart (despite the fact that it had been repeatedly stolen, broken and ignored since early 1970).

And so, because both her children had been invited to a *How to Train Your Sibling* course run by the RSPCA, it came to be that this magnificently kind and loving aunt found herself with the first free Saturday afternoon she'd enjoyed since her own conception. And, typically, the blessed aunt thought nought of herself and her own obvious emotional needs, but rather of her sister's two-year-old son who went by the name Prince No.

Vroom Vroom went her car as the amazing aunt drove a very long way to collect little Prince No from the mansion he shared with his mother and father and their ridiculously large-breasted Swedish *au pair*. 'Lucky I'm minding Prince No today and giving the *au pair* a day off,' said the aunt. 'Carrying those breasts around all day long must make her quite exhausted!

And so the aunt arrived. 'Woof woof' went Woof, the

bull terrier guard dog. 'Knock, knock' tapped the aunt upon the mansion's big front door. 'Nothing,' went the door as it smoothly opened (because the door had been fitted by a rare craftsman who not only knew what on earth he was doing but had also turned up to do the job on the very day that he said he would!). 'My, you're well hung!' said the gentle aunt as she gazed upon the door.

'Hell low Aunt,' said the father of little Prince No – a right pretentious git car-salesman, who'd made a mozza selling thinly disguised undrivable vehicles to people who trusted him. 'My, don't you look tired! I'll just get the fruit of my loins for you.' And with that there was a very loud 'Nooooooo'.

'He's so looking forward to spending the day with his favourite aunt,' said the wonderful aunt's sister.'

'And I,' said the beatific aunt, 'am thrilled to have a day with Prince No.'

'Oh, do try not to call him that!' entreated the sister. 'His therapist says No is far too negative. We tried Yes, but thought it was too much pressure. And so now, if you don't mind, we'd rather call him Maybe.'

'You'll never change the little fella,' said the git.

'I bet I can,' mused the aunt. And with that one phrase, the once god-like-deity aunt joined the massive seething throng of deluded women throughout history who thought that they could change a male.

The pathetic aunt revved the engine of her old *Peugeot de merde* (which she had once also thought would probably improve under her influence) and watched little Prince No kiss his Mummy and Daddy. Then the big-bosomed *au pair* successfully hugged Prince No goodbye, without either crushing his clothes or killing him, and then the aunt and Prince No drove off.

'Do you want to go to the zoo?' asked the aunt.

'No,' said little Prince No.

'Want to go for a swim?' 'No.' 'A walk in the park?' 'No.' 'Want to play on the swings?' 'Noooooooooo.' 'Would you like an ice-cream, a packet of chips, a huge box of popcorn?' 'No, no, no!'

'Would you like to drive a tractor, meet a fireman, fly a fighter jet, play footy, have a small snooze, pull the legs off an ant, blow up a building? Would you please tell me what you want to do?' sobbed the aunt.

'I want to say NO,' said No. 'But before I do,' No continued articulately, 'let me tell you a tale. Once upon a time there were three beautiful princesses who were all to marry. But each princess fell in love with a man not for who he was, but who he could be. The princesses' parents, displeased with this, announced that their daughters would choose their future husbands by each firing an arrow from the palace balcony and then seeing which male it landed nearest. Well, the first princess's arrow landed by a farmer who was good and honest and kind. The second princess's arrow landed by a financier who was a dick-wit but good looking and rich. And the third princess's arrow landed by a frog. "Oh, no!" said the youngest princess. "I can't marry a frog!" But her parents said she must. And so it came to be that the third princess married a frog.'

'And then what?'

'Nothing,' said No.'

'But surely the frog turned into a benevolent handsome prince; that's what always happens!'

'No,' said Prince No, 'the frog just stayed a frog.'

Titanic love

I've just finished watching *Titanic* on video. Uh huh. Have you ever wondered why Leonardo DiCaprio had to die in it? Tell me that you haven't watched Leonardo help Kate Winslet and her heaving bosom clamber atop that piece of floating wood and not wondered why the hell Leonardo didn't climb out of the ice-cold water and hop aboard his own bit of debris. Duh! Tell me you haven't watched blue Leonardo paddling valiantly amongst the icicles and not thought, 'Stop being such a drama queen! You don't have to prove to Kate that you're macho any more, for God's sake you've already had sex with her!'

In a previous, more optimistic draft of the script, absolutely everyone survived. But research suggested most audiences felt you couldn't have a theme song sung by Celine Dion and not have someone die for it. So a further draft was commissioned that had only a few ugly people dying and Kate Winslet. Research proved however that were Kate's character to die in *Titanic* no one, including Leo's character, would actually give a damn.

And so it came to be that Leonardo volunteered to die, no, not volunteered . . . begged. And have you ever wondered why? Well, let's imagine what would have happened if Leonardo, that charming, free-spirited, rootin'-tootin', 'king of the world' had survived.

Of course, one option, after arriving in New York, is that Leo would have dumped Kate because she's willy teasing and pretentious. And then Leo would have grown some facial hair. He would have made a mozza selling his story to *60 Minutes*, taken a starring role in *Riverdance*, slept with the entire cast, and then lost his fortune gambling.

Alternatively, Kate may have done a nude TV ad for car suspension, opened a jewellery shop, and dumped Leo because he's a SNAG – seriously nauseating amorphous git.

Broken-hearted, each may then have called upon a service I have endorsed in print before: Heart Help (formerly known as Loser Line). You just call them when you're missing your ex and they'll send someone over straight away, ready to re-enact the essence of your relationship and remind you of just how good it is that your partner has gone.

For female customers: 'They start by saying they'll ring, and then they don't. They say they'll arrive at an agreed time, and then they won't. And when they do arrive they don't notice how attractive you look, and comment instead on some sexy new chick in the office. They walk straight to the fridge and complain there's no food, flick on the television and put their feet on the coffee table, fart, say they don't want to go to dinner any more and suggest you order a pizza. They grunt a quick bonk before the food arrives, have a shower, flood the bathroom, eat the pizza, drink a beer, fall asleep on the couch, and then leave. All for just $50.'

For males missing lost girlfriends they offer a similar service. 'When you ring she asks you what's wrong. When you say, "Nothing," she asks if you still love her. When you say, "Of course I do," she cries and says you're just saying that. You suggest dinner, she says she's not hungry, she orders a salad and spends the meal picking the best bits from your plate. You drop her home, she starts to cry and suggests you don't find her sexually attractive any more, you say you do and would like to make love, and she tells you she can't just suddenly be turned on like a machine and would like to talk about your relationship. You watch *Pretty Woman* on video. She makes you pat her cat while she talks about her lonely misunderstood childhood, she says she thinks she'd like to have a baby, she starts to cry, you try to kiss her, her PMT kicks in, she says she never wants to see you again and throws you out of the house. Two minutes later she rings you on the car phone, says she misses you and feels like making luuuuuuurv. So you buy flowers, drive back and knock on the door . . . but she's fast asleep . . . dreaming of that ugly quirky guy in *Friends*.'

But let's imagine Leo and Kate did stay together. Let's imagine that this was true and perfect Freedom Furniture love. Would they have got married (fabulous wedding, just like in a movie), had three children (so much more fashionable now than two), stopped having sex (because they respect each other too much), and then died of old age wearing the sorts of equestrian outfits people who can't even ride a horse wear when they go to the polo? Yes, quite possibly.

Aaaaaaaaaaaaaaargh!

I wouldn't be surprised if Leo planted the iceberg.

life wasn't meant to be sleazy

En flight to Denver he forces a cough to try to hide the silent but deadly fart he's just let fly. 'Are you enjoying the ride?' he says. 'No,' I reply.

The entire Argentinean polo team is on this plane but I'm sitting next to the farter from Des Moines.

I'd stupidly opened a conversation before take-off ('Excuse me, I think you're sitting in my seat.') and now I suspect he genuinely believes we're in the courting stages of a full-blown relationship. 'Why do dogs lick their goolies?' he woos intimately. 'Because they can!' (Dog genital jokes already! It must be love.)

We reach cruising altitude and I don't want to speak so I stick my head in an air sick bag. 'Oh phew, are you gonna spew?' he bellows. 'Here take a throw into this.' (N.B. It's my handbag.) And with that he rises, mammoth-like, looks around, tumbles back to his seat, and says, 'There's nothing better available, guess I'll stay with you.' (Oh thank heavens somebody wants me! My mother *will* be pleased.)

I pretend I've gone deaf. (I'd pretend I don't speak English, but I think this bloke would find that exotic.) Instead of shutting up he just speaks louder. 'Did you hear about the bloke who ends up on a desert island living with

Cindy Crawford? All they do is have sex. But after four months he starts to get depressed so she asks what she can do to help. And he says could you put on my shirt, pants and hat, draw a moustache on your face and then start walking around the island. So she sets off and he sets off in the other direction and they meet up after five minutes. He rushes up to her, slaps her on the back and says, "Oh Schweppes, I've forgotten the punchline!" ' *

Space invasion. He clutches my arm through the turbulence and orders drinks for 'us'. I am flabbergastingly repulsed but so legendarily, hopelessly reticent about hurting a bloke's feelings that at this rate I could end up marrying the git.

I'm starting to feel pretty sick. Could this be due to lack of oxygen or is it just that my course in positive thinking has finally paid off and I'm about to spontaneously combust.

We land and he says pontificatingly, 'The thing about Mary in *There's Something About Mary* is that she doesn't wear any underwear throughout the entire fillum!' And then he continues, 'Did you hear about the blonde who was driving to the Warner Brothers theme park when she saw a sign saying "Hollywood left" so she turned around and drove home?' He laughs, he farts, he makes a squishy-nose as though suggesting the 'doer' were me, and I grab my baggage, K.O. some Herbalife consultants (accidentally), and start to run, run, run free . . . free from the farter in 26D.

In customs I see him getting along famously with a woman who appears to be a deaf-mute. I'm briefly jealous because, as my mother would say, 'It's all very well to be a smart-arse cynic, Gretel, but people like those two over there get married and become self-funded retirees.'

I dizzily catch a cab and by the tibe I arribe ad by hotel I hab really god the ships. By doze is clogged, by earz are blogged and I hab a headegg. I go to by hodel roob, swaddow a tab-led, ad as the bedication kicks in, pood two dollars id the slot to bake the bed vibrate erotically but instead it bakes the bed lurch and tilt quite erratically.

I fall asleep and dream I'm having sex for the very first time. The dream lasts four seconds and then I'm woken by a thunderous explosion . . . (it's EXACTLY like the first time I had sex).

I call Wupert at weception to ask if the hotel's been bombed and he scweems. So I swallow another couple of cold tablets and ring 911. I'm put on hold, listen to the music and have a little dance until there's another muffled explosion. I throw myself under the bed . . . and miss. Thepillsarestartingtokickinand I can hear a man laughing. Wow! And I don't even have my clothes off.

Then I hear a voice that sounds like a burp say, 'So baby, why do dogs lick their goolies?' Oh no! It's the farter from Des Moines in the room next door, apparently successfully seducing someone or other even more desperate than, for example, *moi*.

'Oh baby,' I hear him say. 'Get a load of this!' Is he nude and doing 'Oooh baby, oh baby, check out my playstation!' It's so reeeeeevolting I resolve never to have sex again (which is a bit like a beggar promising not to eat caviar), and on and on he goes until finally I hear him yell, 'So are you enjoying the ride?'

'No,' I reply through the wall.

(*'You'll never guess who I'm sleeping with!')

true wisdom only

really comes when

your breasts are the

past tense of pert